Set Me Free

WALTER MOORE

ADULLAM HOMES
HOUSING ASSOCIATION LIMITED
West Bromwich

First published 1980
This edition 2007
Reprinted with corrections 2011

Published by
Adullam Homes Housing Association Limited
Walter Moore House, 34 Dudley Street
West Bromwich B70 9LS

ISBN: 978 0 9557355 0 9

Book design and production for the publisher by
Bookprint Creative Services, <www.bookprint.co.uk>
Printed in Great Britain.

I dedicate this book to Alec Webb,
and all my many friends in the Probation Service,
in humble appreciation of their help and advice which has
always been so readily available, and so freely given,
and to my wife Dorothy, for her love, patience and
forbearance over sixty years without which
this book could never have been written.

CONTENTS

FOREWORD

Welcome to an astonishing book; the story of a man who, having retired from a successful business career, was drawn into engaging with some of the most hard to reach groups in society; a man who created, in Adullam, a Housing Association that continues to be at the forefront in providing for the neediest and most marginalised. Walter Moore's personal account of his work among the convicts, drug abusers and alcoholics of 1970s Birmingham was first published over twenty five years ago, and it is very timely that it is reprinted today.

Both Walter and the organisation he founded, take a back seat in these pages. His passion was for the people whose broken lives he sought to put back together again, and it is their stories, sometimes tragic and sometimes triumphant, that he sets to the fore. He saw himself and Adullam as simply tools in the service of God to achieve that end.

In the years since he wrote, the Housing Association movement has grown rapidly and matured into a highly professional service. At the same time, perhaps inevitably, some of the passion and sense of personal mission of that previous generation has been dissipated. This book should be required reading for all who want to recover the motivation for why Social Housing matters; it reminds us that the tenants and residents of Housing Associations are real human beings with powerful stories to tell, not mere statistics on a spreadsheet.

Walter's story is a story of faith. It is God who calls him to this unlikely work, and God who underpins all that Walter will achieve. At the time he was writing I was getting to know Christian housing projects in Cambridge and then Birmingham. Over the intervening years it has been my privilege to meet countless men and women working in Social Housing or serving on the boards of Housing Associations out of a strong sense of Christian calling. In this I have found, time and time again, that same openness to work with individuals, whatever their histories or detractions, that Walter Moore possessed. Whilst all of our journeys are individual, many will find echoes of what inspires and sustains us in the chapters that follow. As Walter writes, it is not enough for us to preach and provide, we must be characterised by love. May we take that to heart.

Walter ends his account by remarking that the social problems which have led to his work are on the increase. A quarter of a century later, levels of imprisonment and of the abuse of drugs and alcohol are still steadily growing; the challenge with which he left his readers in 1980 was that the church must accept or lose its credibility; it is as relevant today as when he wrote it. In his memory, let this book reissue that challenge today.

David Walker
Bishop of Dudley
Lent 2007

SET ME FREE

Save me by your power, O God;
  set me free by your might!

Hear my prayer, O God;
  listen to my words!

Proud men are coming to attack me;
  cruel men are trying to kill me –
  men who do not care about God.

But God is my helper,
  The Lord is my defender.

May God use their own evil to punish
  my enemies.

He will destroy them because he is
  faithful.

I will gladly offer you a sacrifice, O Lord;
  I will give you thanks
  because you are good.

You have rescued me from all my
  troubles,
    and I have seen my enemies defeated.

Psalm 54 – Good News Bible

CHAPTER ONE

FACE TO FACE WITH THE UNKNOWN

My telephone seldom rang at 8 a.m. and I picked up the receiver with some foreboding. It was old Jack, the Warden at our Newhaven Hostel in the heart of Birmingham's red light district of Balsall Heath.

"You'd better come down 'ere, gaffer."

I feared the worst. Jack was never one to call for assistance if he could handle a situation himself. He was a tough character.

"What's the matter, Jack?"

"It's Bill and Art, they 'ad a bust-up last night, and Art broke a glass on 'im. There's a trail of blood from the lounge to 'is bedroom, and now Bill reckons 'e's goin' to kill 'im."

I knew both men. Bill had just finished a two year sentence for breaking a policeman's jaw, and Arthur had an unenviable record of violence. Both were young, strong and hefty, and men of action rather than words. At seventy years of age, I did not relish becoming too involved in their hostilities.

"Where are they now, Jack?" I was just stalling.

"Art's in 'is room, and Bill's waiting for 'im to come out."

13

I had always impressed upon Jack the need for faith in God in any crisis, and the present situation certainly assumed that dimension.

"Look, Jack," I said, "I'll get down on my knees now, where I am, and pray that God will intervene, and you must do the same."

"You'd better come down 'ere and pray, gaffer," he replied. Jack was always intensely practical. He never minced his words, and I felt the sting of his rebuke. He needed at least the moral support of my presence.

"All right, Jack, I'll be right over."

I was very conscious of my own incompetence to cope with such a situation, and before leaving the house, I did get down on my knees and humbly confessed my inadequacy, and committed the matter to God. I was at the hostel within half an hour, and I felt a sense of relief at least to find that there was neither police car nor ambulance in evidence. The place seemed unusually calm. When I went into Jack's room at the rear I found he was his usual taciturn and imperturbable self.

"What's happened, Jack?"

"Oh, Art came out and said 'e were sorry, and they shook 'ands and went out together."

He spoke as if it were the natural sequence of events. Old Jack seldom showed any emotion, but my heart went up in thankfulness to our Almighty God. The dispute between the men had apparently been simmering for some time, and on the previous night Bill had returned somewhat the worse for drink, and in a provocative mood had started an argument with Arthur, who had spent the evening indoors and was quite sober. Bill was the more powerful of the two, and was content to use his fists, but

Art was the more mentally alert, and a glass broken in the struggle provided him with an effective weapon. Bill had to retire to his room, his face streaming with blood from an ugly gash. Morning found Bill in a bitter mood, ready to wreak vengeance, and he was not squeamish in his methods. He told Jack that he was going to "do 'im and scarper". We neither of us knew just what had transpired. Arthur was never one to funk a fight, and he would never readily apologise, but we had a God who answered prayer, a God who had the solution to every crisis, however impossible it appeared.

Newhaven existed on little but faith. Faith in the impossible. I had bought it for a modest sum, as it was due for early demolition under a slum clearance scheme. We desperately needed some sort of accommodation for the people we were striving to help, the alcoholics, and drug-addicts, and the homeless ex-offenders, like Bill and Arthur. There were seventeen rooms but only three were occupied when we took over. Some of the rooms were half-furnished, but others were filled with lumber and rubbish, and generally in a state of neglect.

My first reaction was one of dismay and consternation. Where could I find the staff for such an undertaking? I was associated at the time with one or two organisations concerned with the homeless, but I had acted independently in the purchase of this property. Then "out of the blue" came old Jack. I had first met him in the drug-addiction and alcoholic unit of All Saints Hospital, in the rather seedy Winson Green area of Birmingham. He had been fished out of the River Severn after a determined attempt at suicide, the result of a bout of excessive drinking. Jack had had a chequered career, spending many years in jail, including a long sentence for manslaughter, after killing a man in a drunken brawl. He had, nevertheless, some sterling qualities, and was a very competent tradesman. After much persuasion he had agreed to go to a Christian rehabilitation centre on a farm near Birmingham, and my first impulse was to persuade him to return. Jack however had made up his mind.

"I'm not going back," he assured me. "If you can't let me stay, I'll be sleeping under the 'edgerow tonight."

When Jack made up his mind, no power on earth could change it.

"But you can see how the place is, Jack," I protested. "It's a shambles."

"Leave it to me, gaffer," he said. "I'll be caretaker, or warden, or whatever you want."

He was as good as his word. The following day I was amazed at the transformation. Rooms were swept and mopped out, furniture rearranged, and where sheets and bedding were available the beds had been made up. A group of students from Birmingham University voluntarily undertook urgent decorations, and within three weeks we were ready to receive our first "guests". I suggested to Jack that to economise on labour, we had better offer just "bed and breakfast", but he insisted on "full board".

"But what about all the cooking?" I queried.

"I'll look after it," he assured me.

"And what about your wages?"

"I don't want none. Just you get the grub, and leave it to me."

Jack was as good as his word. One by one, our guests arrived, some from the jails, and some from the streets. He cooked meals, made beds, cleaned and scrubbed, and generally kept law and order. He was indefatigable. For two years he ruled his empire with a quiet dignity, and a firm hand. He would often bring me a portion of his pension and insist that I put it towards expenses. I felt humbled by his devotion and dedication. He was God's choice for our "Cave of Adullam", and only Jack could have controlled such a medley of ex-offenders, alcoholics and vagrants.

Every man had his own room. It gave him a sense of independence and identity. I had seen so much of the hostel-type accommodation, with its dormitories and communal rooms, its list of rules and instructions. So many of these men had been pushed around, and regimented, and made to conform to a way of life which inhibited self-reliance. Old Jack understood this only too well. We allowed the maximum amount of freedom compatible with accepted standards of behaviour. There was a common dining-room, and a lounge, and generally the atmosphere was friendly and homely, but everyone had the privilege of retiring to their own rooms at any time if they so wished.

If any dispute arose, it was usually efficiently controlled by Jack, who was liked and respected, and possibly a little feared. One man did fall foul of his authority, and was told to go. In a furious temper he immediately went to his room and put a lighted candle under the mattress, surrounding it with anything inflammable he could find, and left. Two hours later, worried and distressed, he went to the Police Station and confessed what he had done. Just after midnight, Jack was awakened from his sleep by the sirens of the fire engines, and a hammering on the door.

When Jack opened the street door two uniformed men were outside.

"Where's the fire?" they demanded.

"What fire?" Jack was a little bewildered.

"We've only got gas fires."

"Is there a chap called Peter living here?"

"There is, do you want 'im?" Jack did not like men in uniform, and he was becoming hostile.

"We'd like to see his room."

"At this time o' night?"

The officer thought it better to placate him.

"We've reason to believe it might be on fire." He said.

Reluctantly, Jack led them to Peter's bedroom, and opened the door. There seemed nothing amiss. They looked under the bed. A candle was just under the mattress, and a small blackened area, about the size of a penny, indicated that it had been lit, but a gust of wind, or some other agency, had extinguished it. The fireman described it as a providential escape, but to me it once again indicated the hand of the Almighty, and his care. Peter was in court on the following day, but we spoke in his defence, and he was allowed to return to us.

The area around Newhaven was depressed and often derelict, and Jack asked us to get a dog in case we had nocturnal intruders. We managed to secure a large black Labrador from the local dogs' home. Jack and Prince soon became inseparable. It probably enhanced Jack's authority, as together they proved a formidable foe, and a deterrent to any would-be attacker. On one occasion however, Prince decided to assert his independence, and taking advantage of an open door, he took a solitary stroll. Whether he was distracted by the allurements of the opposite sex, or whether he just lost his bearings, we do not know, but he got himself hopelessly lost. He was taken by some kind person to the Police Station, and suffered the indignity of a night in the cells. It was a very distressed Jack who finally located him, and we managed to bring the wanderer home, a little shamefaced, but obviously relieved.

"You're the odd man out, now, gaffer," said Jack, when we arrived back.

"Why, Jack?"

"Even the perishin' dog's been in the nick now," he said wryly.

We had a young married couple at Newhaven, and Jack was delighted when our first baby arrived. He was very anxious to be godfather to the child, and he asked me about the ceremony. I had some misgivings. Both parents had been in trouble, and although they had made excellent progress I doubted whether they would be prepared for such an occasion, and whether it would be meaningful to them. By now, we had a Committee, and most of my colleagues were of Anglican persuasion. I told Jack that I was not personally in favour of christening, and preferred dedication, and baptism by immersion after they had reached an age of discretion, but I said it must be the choice of the parents as to whether the baby was christened or 'dedicated'. The following morning Jack came into our little office.

"We ain't 'avin the bab' christened," he said, abruptly. There was a glint of steel in his grey eyes which defied contradiction.

"We want 'er desecrated." Dear old Jack. He was always loyal.

A fairly large room had been set apart for Sunday evening Service, and for worship. Nobody was ever under any pressure to attend, but many of the men did come on Sunday evenings for a few hymns and a short address. They usually chose their own hymns, and one would lead in a short and simple prayer. I was rather taken aback, however, when one of the young men asked me if I could "cast out devils". I enquired the circumstances, and he explained he wanted to bring along a young man who was convinced that he was "demon-possessed". I had to confess my ignorance of such matters, apart from my knowledge of the Scriptures, but he said that the young fellow had been dabbling in "demon-worship", and was tormented by an evil spirit. He was terrified to pass a church, and was in a very distressed state. I agreed that he should be allowed to come along on the Sunday evening. The meeting had already started when they brought him in, and he sat in a chair, looking distraught, and very frightened. He was given a hymn book, but he gripped it as if his life depended on keeping it closed. As we sang a hymn he became increasingly distressed, and when someone started to pray, he leapt up and made for the door. I followed him out and found him in the passage, sobbing.

"Do something ... do something ..." he cried, piteously.

I took him to a small, unoccupied room, and sat him down. Then I began to sense something of the horror of the obscene thing which possessed him. I would have liked to call for help, but I knew that no such help was available. I was face-to-face with something unknown and intangible. There were beads of sweat on the young man's forehead, and he was trembling violently.

"Help me," he cried again, and gave an involuntary groan.

I felt afraid, and helpless. I had read about such things, but this was a direct confrontation with the powers of darkness.

"Lord," I cried, "Thou art the Almighty God. Our trust is in Thee alone. Whatever this evil is, by Thy power deliver us."

I knelt opposite the young man, who was still shaking and sobbing, and I put my hand on his.

"Try and pray, just cry to God," I told him.

"I can't, I can't . . ." he almost shrieked.

"Take the name of Jesus on your lips," I persisted.

"I can't . . ." he almost spat the words at me.

Then it happened. As if the words were wrenched from his inmost soul.

"Jesus . . . Jesus . . ." he cried, as if in mortal agony.

There followed another bout of sobbing which gradually subsided.

"How do you feel now?" I asked. His voice was almost a whisper.

"I feel weak," he said, "but it's gone. IT'S GONE, I'm all right . . . I'm all right . . ."

My wife had opened the door, and joined us, and together we all lifted our hearts to God in thankfulness and praise. How mightily he comes to our aid, when our soul cries out in distress. The young man came to a meeting in our own home on the following day, and joined lustily in the hymns. He was completely delivered.

> *Jesus* the name high over all
> In heaven, or earth or sky,
> Angels and men before him fall,
> *and devils fear and fly.*

We had often sung the hymn, but only in the stark reality of confrontation with the unknown, unseen evil, with a consciousness of one's utter impotence, did we know something of the glorious triumph of that last line.

Newhaven taught us many lessons, but it confirmed me in my conviction that the majority of society's misfits will respond to a sincere concern for their welfare if we do not attempt to impose upon them our own concepts of conduct. The counsellor and do-gooder will be humoured and exploited, and officialdom tolerated and placated. Barriers have been built which are hard to break down, but they can be broken down, and so often we find a soft interior. There is usually a vulnerable spot in their defence mechanism. Old Jack was amazingly perceptive in his assessment of our men. He had a term of contempt for the scrounger, while on the other side of the coin, the meddling "do-gooder" he would refer to as "them mushes". He always had a ready sympathy with real distress.

I once met a wizened little old man in the lounge, and I asked Jack who he was. I knew he had not been officially admitted.

"'E's a bloke I knew in the nick, come along to see me," Jack explained, in a tone of voice I knew did not invite further enquiry. It was quite by accident that I later learnt that Jack had found him "skippering"* in a derelict house, and had invited him to stay at the hostel. He was mentally retarded and Jack had taken him in, bathed him, removed his verminous garments and burnt them, and had clothed him in his own underwear and socks, and found him a suit and shoes. He had fed him from his own table, before

---

* Sleeping rough

the old chap was finally taken to hospital. Jack hated to be found out in these little acts of tenderness. He seemed ashamed to reveal any chink in the armour of his tough exterior.

Such incidents have happened so often, and given a momentary glimpse into the inner soul of even the most hardened wrong-doer. The longer I live and work among these people, the more I become convinced of the ultimate triumph of love. No maudlin sentimentality, but a genuine caring and understanding. Let there be no misconception. The child is, or should be, taught that punishment is the inevitable consequence of transgression, and as adults, if we have failed to learn this lesson due to inadequate instruction, or to our own self-will, it must be drilled home with great severity and stringency.

Old Jack had taken his share of punishment. He had accepted it with stoicism, and without any apparent resentment. His years in jail had left their mark, but there was an innate tenderness which he would always hide behind a brusque and aggressive manner. He had a wholesome respect for our judicial system, and had little time for the petty thief who whined and protested that he had been wrongly convicted. He was convinced that corporal punishment should be administered to the people who used violence to the elderly, or to the weak. He had his own rigid code.

At Newhaven, we believed that punishment must follow crime, not as revenge, but as it's natural consequence. We recognised, however, that having completed the sentence, the man (or woman) had paid the debt, and must not be stigmatised or harried by the record of it. It is then that they need our compassion and our understanding.

There is surely no more lonely person than the homeless ex-prisoner, as he steps out of those massive gates into a "free" world. He is unwanted. He knows that if he were knocked down and killed by a passing car, nobody would really care, nobody would shed a tear. He sees the world rushing by, each person intent on their own business, most of them returning at the end of the day to a welcome, a meal and a warm fireside. Whether the ex-prisoner's mood is one of defiance, or just hopelessness and sullen despair, he drifts into the nearest pub to purchase a friendly chat at the cost of a few drinks, and ultimately to seek oblivion. Maybe he'll have a little money left for a bed at some cheap "hotel" or lodging house. Who cares?

There are, of course, many institutions and societies that are geared to this type of problem, ready to give temporary help. We have welfare workers, social services and a very helpful and efficient probation service. They are all redolent, however, of the same "Authority" which has been dominating and controlling our ex-prisoner's life, and he doesn't like the smell.

We try to remember that the people we so glibly label as "ex-offenders" are often just ordinary folk like ourselves, who have maybe been deprived of parental care, and have been thrust out upon a hard and uncompromising world without the love and restraining influence of the family circle.

Here is the real place for action by the Christian church. Are we content to wait for them to attend our place of worship, to hear our preaching? Or shall we meet them at the prison gates, with a word of welcome, and the offer of a friendly fireside, and a home? The Scriptures tell us that our Lord, on many occasions, met the physical need of the outcast before he ministered to the soul. He healed ten lepers, and only one returned to give thanks, and to seek the greater gift of eternal life. He knew the heartache and disappointment, but surely the one who returned made it all worthwhile.

At Newhaven, we also had our disappointments, but we tried to meet the need, and many lives were changed. We gave these men a measure of independence. They had a room of their own, a place of security, but I know that we were not satisfying their most urgent need, a home of their own. A place where no prying warden could say "lights out". Homelessness and rootlessness are soul-destroying. They undermine self-respect. They are degrading and humiliating, and they will defeat the resolution of a discharged prisoner to seek a better life.

The object of the ensuing pages is to tell of our earnest, if feeble efforts to meet this demand, and to look at the lives of some of the people we tried to help. They have all agreed that I should tell their story, but in some cases we have used other names to preserve their anonymity. Many have paid the price of man's imperfect justice. Some have passed beyond man's jurisdiction to a greater Judge, to an Almighty One who knows our weaknesses, and remembers that we are dust.

I am often asked why I spend so much time and labour in helping these seemingly undeserving folk when there is so much need elsewhere.

"Well, you see," I tell them, "I was once homeless myself, and I realise that there, but for the Grace of God, go I."

CHAPTER TWO

CLOTHED IN SACKCLOTH

The Mission Sunday School had just begun, and some thirty children between the ages of five and fourteen were giving their own individual rendering of "What a Friend we have in Jesus". One of the voluntary helpers went over to a girl of about twelve years who was sitting on the front row, and called her aside.

"Mary," she whispered, "whatever is that on your pinafore?"

Mary regarded her with tolerant amusement, surprised at her concern.

"It's a bug," she said, with unaffected nonchalance, and unceremoniously brushed it to the floor, as if unworthy of even a summary execution.

Nottingham, in the early part of the century, had many areas of poverty and slum. None was worse than Narrow Marsh, with its labyrinth of courts and alleyways, a hotch-potch of hovels, lodging-houses and brothels, with their lines of washing slung in gay disarray across the yards. Children of all ages, ragged, dirty and unkempt, ran barefoot across the street. Many houses had no water supply, and kettles, buckets and saucepans were filled from a communal street tap.

The hoardings and railways in those days, carried a strident message of hope, "KEATING'S POWDER KILLS BUGS, FLEAS, MOTHS, BEETLES" but in Narrow Marsh you just couldn't afford such refinements. In any case the advertiser never mentioned their biggest enemy, lice, either from a Victorian sense of gentility and reticence, or a consciousness of its inadequacy against a foe so numerous, and so deeply entrenched. The infestation, along with the poverty and its attendant hunger, was accepted with stoicism and an almost fatalistic indifference, just as you accepted the daily drunken brawls outside the pubs, and the ever-present threat of the patrolling policeman. You expected "Dad" to come home plastered on a Saturday night. You went through his pockets after he had fallen asleep in a drunken stupor, and salvaged maybe an odd shilling or sixpence to buy bread and margarine, and tea and sugar for the week. Then Monday morning, and back to "Uncle's" with any acceptable item of clothing or shoes, to eke out a meagre existence for the rest of the week. It was a way of life, and oddly enough, many survived. Tuberculosis took its terrible toll, and malnutrition so often broke down the defences against malignant disease.

By 1910 the "Marsh" had acquired such an unsavoury reputation that it was decided to rename it Red Lion Street, but to most of us who knew it, it was still the "Marsh". Its squalor remained until the whole area was demolished and rebuilt.

From the industrial area around St. Mary's Church, a flight of narrow stone steps down the face of the rock led into the Marsh, and at the bottom of the steps, around the corner, was a rather nondescript little Mission Hall. It was here that my mother, rather frail, and in her middle forties, marshalled what forces she could muster, in her own private battle against the depravity, the degradation and the despair of the environment. She was well-loved by all who knew her. Mother had had her own share of personal suffering. She had lost two daughters, and my eldest brother, who had been stricken with polio when only six years old, was partially paralysed for the remainder of his life. My father had left home during my early childhood, and Mother had brought up a family of four, single-handed. Some are embittered by adversity, but my mother's sorrows had left her with a sweet serenity of spirit. She was utterly dedicated to the service of her Lord. Mother had been brought up in the elegant seclusion and propriety of a mid-Victorian home, and had always struggled to perpetuate its refinements, but when she was told of the imminent closing down of a slum mission, she stepped into the breach, and into its squalor, armed with little more than a warm compassionate heart.

By three o'clock on a Sunday afternoon, the mission hall was filled with youngsters of all ages, sitting on wooden benches, a bedlam of chattering voices, gurgles and giggles, and an occasional squabble, sometimes demanding the physical separation of battling elements. I shall never know how my mother managed to teach them to sing hymns, tell them Bible stories, play the harmonium, and generally manage to keep some semblance of order. But she did. She always had an ultimate sanction. After the service, the benches were rearranged, and trestle tables erected. A tea of bread, butter, jam and cakes was provided, and any child who had misbehaved was threatened with expulsion without tea. In the best interests of discipline, it was perhaps unfortunate that they knew my mother too well, and were aware that the threat would never be carried out.

Items of clothing, shoes and socks were provided for the more needy cases. She managed to come to an arrangement with the local pawnshops whereby a certain mark was used, which the pawnbroker would recognise and would refuse any article carrying it.

As a boy, it was only on odd occasions that I was allowed to visit the mission, but I still carry a memory of its rather stale smell, the blue banner over the end wall, with its letters in gold, Narrow Marsh Gospel Temperance Mission, and my mother sitting at the harmonium surrounded by half-a-dozen grubby kids, a more mischievous one trying to finger the keys. The shrill and discordant babble of children's voices, ending in a crashing crescendo at the end of the hymn, still remains in my memory. They had so little in life, these youngsters, by present-day standards, but they sang with great gusto.

Sunday evening was the time for visiting the lodging-houses (the euphemism for doss-houses). My mother would be accompanied by one or two helpers, sometimes from the Salvation Army, or Church Army. There would be gospel hymns, and a short talk. On occasions there would be a little ribaldry, but she was well-loved and respected, and any foul language was quickly silenced by the others, and the offender warned in no uncertain terms.

Saturday night at home was invariably "pudding night". We had a copper boiler where about a dozen suet puddings were either steamed or boiled, and my mother, usually with another helper, or one of my brothers, would by some means carry them, on the tram and on foot, the two or more miles to the Marsh. There she would distribute them to the more needy families.

Our home was always "open house" to any itinerant evangelist or preacher or any visiting Salvation Army officer, and no one in need was ever turned away without at least the offer of food. My mother would have been the first to disclaim any altruism or self-sacrifice. She had a living faith in God, and what she did was done quietly and unostentatiously, and as the natural sequence to her beliefs. We were brought up on the assurance that God was the Absolute, that the Scriptures were infallible, and that the only thing of consequence was that we should love God "with all our heart, soul, mind and strength, and our neighbours as ourselves". All else was either complementary or inadmissible. There was no compromise, and no alternative. All was subordinated to the one ultimate goal. "Except a man forsake ALL that he hath . . ." My mother carried this out to the letter.

1914 . . . War . . . It was a new and shattering experience, and it changed all our lives. One of my brothers joined the forces, and at the age of sixteen, I left home to learn farming on a farm near Filey, in Yorkshire. My eldest brother, with a paralysed arm and leg, for the first time was able to earn a wage, owing to the shortage of manpower. My other brother was critically wounded in the battle of the Ancre, in 1916. He lost his left arm and received severe shell wounds in the back. He was on the danger list for some time, but gradually recovered. I was called up at the beginning of 1918, and was eventually sent to the Italian front. Demobbed in March, 1919, I returned to the farm.

The Narrow Marsh Mission had deteriorated to such an extent that it was condemned, and closed for demolition.

Soon after my return to the farm, therefore, I received a letter from my mother to say that she was selling our home, with all its contents, and with my two brothers was going to Liverpool to join a missionary enterprise to evangelise the Congo. At first I was resentful, but not surprised. I had to acknowledge her complete sincerity and dedication. After the stark realism of the war, we had no stomach for the artificiality and urbane responsibility of post-war Edwardian England. My brother had been rewarded by a "grateful country" with a pension of twenty-five shillings a week. We had come back to a land "fit for heroes to live in" and to disillusionment, so we were looking for larger horizons. In spite of my early opposition, I finally decided to leave the farm, and join them. My family, and a number of Christian friends from Birmingham and Liverpool pooled their resources, and took over a large house in Breckside Park, in the Anfield district of Liverpool. We had no immediate specific objective, except to live a "life of faith", with the ultimate purpose of evangelising the Congo, or wherever God should lead. It was our first "Cave of Adullam".

The leader of the group, John Chesterman, had just returned from the Congo, after the death of his wife on the mission field. He had a daughter, Dorothy, the same age as myself. We had met before when fourteen years of age, and had regarded each other with a remote tolerance amounting to indifference. Now we looked at each other with an awakened interest, and after a brief courtship married at the age of twenty-one. Our "wedding breakfast" consisted of bread, margarine and chips, with weak tea, and no miracle to turn it into wine. We had no wedding gifts, no home and no prospects by all accepted standards. Our marriage has already lasted nearly sixty years.

Many lessons were learned during our two years at
Breckside Park. We learned "how to abound, and how to
suffer need", with the "need" usually more common than
the "abounding". We learned the real meaning of "sacrificial giving", as all our most treasured possessions had to
be offered on the altar of common need. We found that
when we had nothing left to give, God moved in a mirac-
ulous way. While we often had to do with only one meal
a day, we never had to go without food. We always had
what we needed, but seldom what we wanted. It was a
hard school, but the lessons were of incalculable value in
later life. The prospects of a missionary expedition to the
Congo, or elsewhere, became more and more remote, and
we finally decided to disband, each to start life anew, with
little else but our faith in God, and a completely readjusted
sense of values.

The farmer near Filey where I had previously stayed,
consented to employ me at thirty-three shillings a week.
The hours were 7 a.m. to 5.30 p.m. each day, including
Sundays. My wife and I managed to rent a small unfur-
nished house at one pound per week, leaving us thirteen
shillings for food, lighting, heating and clothing. How my
wife managed I shall never know, but we never went hungry, even if our main meal consisted of swedes (which we
obtained free from the farm), potatoes, and gravy made
from dripping. Occasionally I was allowed the use of the
farmer's gun, and was able to shoot a rabbit. Then we had
a banquet of real meat, an orgy of unbridled indulgence.
Although life was hard they were happy days for we had
the resilience of youth. A rare visit was sometimes made to
the local cinema (admission twopence), but this soon
became too much of a burden on our weekly budget.

Finally we decided to take the plunge, and move to the industrial Midlands, and after packing all our worldly effects into a solitary suitcase, we rejoined our family in Coventry, and later moved to Birmingham. I had hopes of an engagement on the reporting staff of one of the local papers, but found that any sort of work was almost unobtainable. We soon reached the point where we could no longer afford the usual accommodation, and after getting my wife into the YWCA, my brother and I were compelled to seek refuge in the Salvation Army Hostel in Jamaica Row, at one shilling per night. His pension provided the bare necessities, but the accommodation for our wives had to be paid for, and we were in dire straits. At that time, many of the butchers' shops carried brass signs, with their names beaten in. At a local store, we purchased a tin of black enamel and a small pencil brush, at a total investment of eightpence, and offered to black-in the names on the brass signs in "our new quick-drying black lacquer" for the modest sum of one shilling. We managed quite a reasonable profit on our outlay of capital, and were able, for a time, to augment our depleted funds. Securing a major contract with a butcher on the Soho Road, Handsworth to complete both signs of his corner shop for the princely sum of two shillings and sixpence (12½p in present-day coinage), we became so engrossed in our work we did not notice that the shop had closed, and the staff had gone home. We had been depending on this money for our evening meal, and had to walk back to the hostel – about three miles – without reward for our labours, and no prospect of supper. I returned the following morning to get that money for our breakfast, arriving at the shop on their opening time (as I thought) of nine o'clock. To my horror, I found the butcher's boy in the act of carefully cleaning off the last of our paint.

"What are you doing?" I asked weakly.

"Oh, some silly b . . . has been daubing paint around," he said, rather disdainfully. "I've had to clean it up."

We had no breakfast!

It was some days later, through the intervention of a relative that I managed to get a job. I started with a firm of painting contractors as a "painter's improver", or apprentice, at one shilling per hour. My first week's wages were due on the following Friday, but on the Thursday evening I had just fourpence left, after we had spent the last of my brother's pension on our evening meal. We had no money left for our night's bed. We decided to put our plight to the Salvation Army Captain. I remembered rather nostalgically the old days at home, when so many of their officers had been welcomed and entertained. With some trepidation I knocked on the door of his office.

"Yes?" His tone did not augur well.

I told him of our problem, and explained that I should receive my first week's wages on the morrow. "Could we have beds for the night and we would . . ."

"No. I've seen your sort before. If you haven't any money, you can clear out."

We did not argue. We were homeless, and nearly destitute. For some time we did not feel the full impact of our predicament. Surely there must be somebody, somewhere in the city, to whom we could apply for help in such an emergency! We walked as far as Snow Hill Station, and approached a friendly-looking policeman, and with some embarrassment told him of our dilemma.

"There's the 'ever-open-door'," he suggested, "the casual ward, at Smithfield."

It was a nice way of describing the dreaded "workhouse". He did his best. A thin drizzle was already falling, and it was getting dark. I had a hard day's work ahead the next day. Downcast and humiliated, we trudged through the wet streets to the Poor Law Institution, in what is now the Summerfield hospital. It had a bleak, forbidding exterior. We entered under a stone archway, eerie and almost mediaeval in the darkness, and approached a dimly lit office. Speaking to the officer-in-charge, we explained our case. To our surprise, he was sympathetic and understanding. We knew it was expected of the inmates to carry out certain tasks on the following morning in return for the night's shelter, and we asked about this.

"Don't worry lads," he assured us kindly. "I'll arrange for you to go straight out in the morning. I can see that you're just in a temporary difficulty."

We thanked him. After our previous rebuff, his words were "like rain upon the mown grass". We had to surrender our fourpence, but he assured us that it would be refunded on the following day. I needed it for the tram fare to my job. They took all our clothes, and we were given a hot bath and provided with night attire. It was an inverted sack, with a hole for your head, and two holes for your arms. It was all scrupulously hygienic, but devastating to one's dignity. I glanced at my brother. The stump of his arm, severed in the service of his country, protruded from the sacking twitching, distorted, grotesque. For some moments, I was overwhelmed with resentment and revulsion at the sheer injustice of it all. "A land fit for heroes" . . . this was England, my England.

We were given two blankets and escorted to two-tier bunks, and as we were both very weary all was soon forgotten in sleep.

I had yet to learn that "ALL things work together for good to those who love God" (Romans 8:28).

> Oh to be nothing, nothing,
>   Painful the humbling may be,
> Yet low in the dust I'll lay me,
>   That the world might my Saviour see.

CHAPTER THREE

MY FIRST TIME WITH THE DRUG ADDICTS

That night of desolation at Summerfield left an indelible impression on me. In spite of the privations through which I had passed, I had not yet learned the lesson that "whosoever he be of you that forsaketh not all that he hath he cannot be my disciple" (Luke 14:33), I could not face the final humiliation. Never again would I be placed in such a predicament. I would fight back, and slowly and inexorably I became so utterly absorbed in the struggle that Christ was forced into the background of my thoughts, and my faith was slowly eroded and forgotten. I was gradually estranged from the Christian fellowship I had known for so long. The Scripture, "Demas hath forsaken me, having loved this present world" (2 Timothy 4:10) applied also to my life at this time.

The years between the wars were lean years. The threat of unemployment with its attendant hardships was ever present. One knew that however capable and efficient you might be, another, even better, was ready to step into your place. The employer, faced himself with severe competition, naturally used the situation to his advantage. I had been thrust into a job for which I received no training, and had no particular skill, but I held on grimly, making up in effort and application what I lacked in technique. I soon acquired the drinking habits of my fellow workmen, and as my skill as a tradesman improved, I was frequently sent on out-of-town jobs, where the opportunity of long hours of overtime boosted the wage packet, but where the evening drinking session was part of the accepted routine.

It was 1939, and once again we were at war. At forty, without any special qualifications, I was of little use for active service, but I enlisted in the Civil Defence as an air-raid warden, and also joined the St. John's Ambulance for a period of training. Birmingham soon became a major target for the bombing, and I saw more "active service" than I had with the Forces in the previous war. I had three very narrow escapes after being within twenty yards of an exploding bomb. One was when a direct hit on an air-raid shelter occurred just after I had been inside in the course of my duty, and some thirty people were killed. I realised that I had been near to being plunged into eternity, and I was filled with a deep-seated spiritual unrest. In the midst of death and destruction however, there is inherent in most of us a certain assurance of our own survival, and any upsurge of a struggling conscience was usually assuaged by the sedative effect of alcohol. It always amazed me in later years that I could stand at the brink of eternity with such indifference to the demanding love of my Creator.

In 1945, at the end of the war, and after twenty-three years with this firm, I decided that I must either make a break then, or be compelled to live out my life in this humdrum existence. My wife and I had by now purchased our own home, but it was our only asset. I found a small one-man business offered for sale by a builder and decorator, and my wife agreed to the selling of our home, and throwing our all into the venture. In the existing economic climate it was a great gamble, but her courage and her confidence were the final incentives for me to take the plunge. She also obtained a situation as housekeeper to a local doctor. A private flat of our own was provided, and a garage placed at my disposal, which gave us temporary security. After the purchase of the business had been completed, I found to my dismay that there were considerable undisclosed debts, and the firm was on the verge of bankruptcy. There was little I could do. The previous owner had presented audited accounts, which had been vetted by my own solicitor. Work, however, came in, and I laboured long hours, seven days a week. At the end of six months I had cleared all the debts, and slowly, and often wearily and painfully, a small reserve of capital was built up. Although we tried to concentrate on interior decoration, we were forced to accept all that came our way, and the very hard winter of 1947, with its seemingly unending snow, brought us again to the brink of disaster. We finally weathered the storm, and the following year we had to increase our staff. It had been a hard, uphill, and often gruelling struggle, but we were slowly becoming established. Some of my more affluent friends, shrewdly observing a turn in the tide, offered financial help. I formed a limited company, and with the share capital now available, we were able to obtain larger contracts, where competition was not so acute. This enabled us to move into more spacious premises, with our own flat above the office, and a better standard of living followed. To both of us, however, there was an increasing awareness of the futility of success without an ultimate purpose.

We tried the "broken cisterns". I became a Freemason, and sought some satisfaction in their pseudo-religious rites. It was pleasant company, and their signs and symbols were good fun. There was plenty of drink around and I was becoming increasingly dependent upon it, both morning and evening. A considerable amount of our work was for the local breweries, and this involved daily visits to their licensed houses all over the Midlands, either for estimating or supervision. Invariably I would have a pint of their brew on each visit. Evenings were spent in one of the local hostelries in the company of business friends, usually from about 8.30 p.m. until closing time. The drinking was not excessive, but steady and persistent. It was convivial, but controlled.

By 1950, many essential ingredients in our paint supply were becoming increasingly difficult to obtain, but we had a good contact with a firm in Liverpool, and I paid periodic visits to their depot. My wife and I usually spent the weekend in Merseyside with her brother. He was a devoted and sincere Christian, and was very concerned at our apparent indifference to spiritual affairs. He used all his powers of persuasion, and made every effort to get us to attend the service at his church. He coaxed and cajoled, he pleaded and implored, at every visit. I was compelled to make a further visit in April of that year, and I knew that he would return to the attack.

"I'm sick of being preached at," I told my wife, in the hope that she might suggest staying at an hotel.

"They'd be so disappointed," she protested. I knew that I should have to accept the inevitable.

It was Sunday morning, and the barrage was turned on.

"You'll enjoy it," my brother-in-law said. My wife took me aside quietly.

"Let's go this once," she pleaded, "just to please him."

He assured me that the service would be over just after twelve o'clock, and I reflected that the pubs would then be open. I gave way.

It was the most momentous decision of my life.

The service was held in a small church hall on the Belvedere Road, near Princes Park, in an area of rather large, but dilapidated houses, relics of Liverpool's bygone days of commercial prosperity. The seats were wooden benches, and a raised platform at one end served as a pulpit.

It was all very informal and friendly, with hymns and prayers in which the congregation joined. There was a fervour and a spontaneity in their worship which impressed me. The minister, Robert Raine, a tall well-built man of about forty years, had a powerful voice, and an almost unconscious air of authority. We sang the hymns, and listened to the prayers, and I made furtive glances at my watch. Then the minister gave a short address on the portion of Scripture which he had read. I was prepared for a period of boredom, but out of courtesy decided to pay some semblance of attention. My eyes were soon riveted on his face. It seemed to be illumined with an indefinable aura of joy and peace. I had an uncanny sensation that he was speaking to me personally, and yet I knew that he was a complete stranger, and could have had no prior knowledge of my coming. He spoke of the eternal love of God for the penitent sinner, and of the boundless mercy which could reach out to even those who had continually rejected Him. Surely he meant me! "Lord, and can it ever be, Mercy still reserved for me?" Could an Almighty Creator still be concerned for me, who had rejected and flouted Him, who had so miserably failed Him?

The minister's penetrating eyes now seemed to be directly focused on me.

"Isn't it wonderful, isn't it wonderful," he was saying.

My past years came before me like a nightmare re-lived. Could the past indeed be yet forgiven?

"Isn't it wonderful?" he repeated, as if in answer to my unspoken cry. It was the Holy Spirit speaking to my inmost soul. The defences were down. I had always abhorred any exhibition of emotion, but I bent down with my hands covering my head, tears welling up and streaming down my face. I did not respond to any appeal. I did not go to the penitent form. I left the service without any-one being aware of what had taken place. I went in with indifference, I came out broken and humble before my God. I entered with incredulity, I left knowing that God *lived* and *loved*.

"Isn't it wonderful?" I kept repeating to myself. To my astonishment I found that my wife had had a similar expe-rience. Our whole life and outlook were changed from that day, but neither my brother-in-law nor the minister knew until months later. On the drive home we discussed the many changes involved. There was no hesitation in our decision to completely renounce our old way of life. It was made so much easier by the realisation that both of us were equally determined in our resolution, and I deeply sympathise with the husband or wife or indeed any mem-ber of a family who has to stand alone. We know, however, that His Grace is indeed sufficient.

It is hard to ruthlessly sever ties of friendship which have been built up over the years. I did not want to stand aloof and isolated, but I knew that with many of my former friends I had no longer a common interest. In conversations, in habits, and in our way of life, there was now a gap which must rapidly widen to a chasm. My first step in our new life was to renounce my association with freemasonry, and to advise my many business colleagues and friends that I should not be meeting them again in the old haunts. I was immediately under intense pressure from many quarters. One of my closest friends was very insistent.

"Come and join us again," he urged me, "and I'll drink lemonade with you."

I knew he meant it, and I deeply appreciated the self-denial it would have involved. My apparently callous refusal of his offer appeared unjustifiable, but I was very conscious of my weakness, and knew how easily I could have reverted to my old ways. I had to be resolute. There could be no compromise. It was not a "holier than thou" attitude, it was just that we were travelling in opposite directions. Either they must come my way (and how I wished they would!), or I must go theirs, and there could be no alternative. Our hopes and aspirations, our sense of values, were now poles apart, and "ne'er the twain could meet".

My wife and I rejoined some of our old fellowship who had been faithful through the years, and they gave us the welcome of the prodigal. We later joined a local church, until the time came for thoughts of retirement in 1966. Sixteen quiet, uneventful years, and with no apparent prospect of any active service beyond passive participation in the affairs of the church.

Apart from my indulgence in alcohol. I had never been involved in drug-addiction, and it came as a complete surprise when I was approached by a member of another church, and asked if I would help in a venture to deal with this problem. Apparently there was a sudden and disquieting outbreak and upsurge of the habit in the Midlands, after being mainly confined to the London area, but apart from lurid accounts in the local press, I knew very little about the problem. My friend outlined a proposal to buy a small farm near Birmingham, and convert it into a centre for rehabilitation of young addicts, after treatment and withdrawal at a hospital. The farm which only consisted of a few acres, had been neglected, but with its house and outbuildings, seemed an ideal centre. It was fairly well isolated, in a rural area, and had obviously a potential for the purpose. Was this the opening of the door for labour in the Lord's vineyard? I was now 67 years of age, and had been prepared to accept the fact that I was too old for active service. However, I agreed to help in any way I could, and we decided to go ahead with the purchase. A committee was formed, and within twelve months the farm was ready for our first "guests".

I eagerly grasped the opportunity offered, and became very enthusiastic. I felt the need to get to know the people with whom we were concerned. I managed to persuade a young colleague, Dan Wooding, now a well-known author and journalist, who was rather more conversant with the situation, to allow me to accompany him on a visit to the drug-addiction unit at All Saints Hospital in Birmingham. He agreed rather reluctantly, as he had grave misgivings about my own reactions, and about the impact I should make on the lads he visited. He suggested that I might talk to some of the alcoholics in the ward, who were considerably older. I was rather apprehensive myself as to what sort of reception I should receive. Should I dress for the part, with casual attire, pullover, jeans, and a bizarre tie? I decided on my usual outfit, a pin-stripe suit, with the traditional white shirt and tie. I wanted to be accepted or rejected for what I was, not for what I might appear to be. The ward was nearly empty. One or two young men were lying on their beds, reading or smoking. Some were talking in a group. I was regarded either with an amused tolerance, or casual indifference. I had expected to see a motley crowd of wild-eyed, distraught folk, grotesque, pale and emaciated; instead I found just ordinary, cheerful youngsters, who responded in a friendly way to my approaches. I was grateful of this. I had feared a tongue-tied embarrassment, but I found conversation easy and relaxed. I had a word with the charge nurse, and he readily agreed to a daily visit, and even placed no restrictions on time, apart from the proviso that my nights did not conflict with the daily routine of the ward.

I was delighted with my first encounter and I came away convinced that if I could establish a mutual confidence, the age barrier could soon be broken down. Surely here was a new enterprise, a new life, a new reason for living. Here was a need which must be met. I was ill-equipped and untrained, and it surely would be presumptuous to assume that I could succeed where others had failed, but I knew now that we had a great and Almighty God, and that the ultimate answer was with Him alone. If I had had a presentiment of the appalling tragedies I should have to face, the broken and shattered lives with which I would come into contact, I might indeed have stood hesitating on the brink of the venture, but I believe I would still have plunged into its chilly waters.

I became involved in the daily life of the ward – and its trail of death. And I soon felt that I was standing helpless at the mouth of hell, with its mad masquerade on the very vortex of the abyss.

CHAPTER FOUR

"I'D DIE FOR HEROIN . . ."

I met Tony shortly after my first visit to the All Saints drug-addiction unit. He was a tall, dark-haired youth of seventeen, quiet, well-spoken, and friendly. His hair was neatly trimmed, and reasonably short. He seemed alert to his surroundings. I sat by his bedside, and we were soon exchanging confidences. He was keen on swimming and rugby, and had been fairly successful in his final school exams. He had a good home, and was on quite good terms with his parents. Yes, he had a sister, and . . . oh yes, he had a girlfriend. He saw me looking at the tiny tell-tale punctures in his forearm. There was no need for concealment . . . here.

"How long have you been on the stuff, Tony?" I asked quietly.

"Nearly a year," he replied, averting his eyes.

He was still very sensitive to the shame of it, and at first was disinclined to talk. I did not press him. There was a natural reserve in his manner, and I knew that any outpouring of his heart must come spontaneously, and without my prompting. For his withdrawal treatment, he was put under heavy sedation, and it was some two weeks later before he could again talk coherently. He spoke, at first, about his family, about his remorse at the way he had distressed and disappointed them, how patient they had been with him, and how he had abused their love and understanding. I could only listen. I could neither sympathise nor condemn. At last I ventured a question.

"How did it all start, Tony?" He hesitated before his reply.

"I've never told anyone," he said at last, "but I'll tell you."

I was grateful for this. I suppose my age helped. I was old enough to be his grandfather. He told me of his first visit to a ballroom.

"It all seemed so exciting," he went on, "with the many lights, and the music, and, of course, the girls. There were five of us, but before long, all my pals were dancing with their girlfriends, and I was alone."

Hesitatingly, he spoke of his shyness with the opposite sex.

"Somehow, I just couldn't date them," he explained. "I couldn't even talk to them."

Apparently, one of his friends, who appeared to be having an uproarious time, chivvied him about it. Tony became more despondent than ever. Probably his crestfallen countenance evoked a little sympathy.

"You need a boost, Tony," his pal told him. "Try one of these."

He gave him a small pill, a potent amphetamine. Tony swallowed it, and before long was sensing the euphoria so symptomatic of the first experiment with the drug. He felt he had acquired a new confidence, and a sense of wellbeing. The old inhibitions disappeared, and with a newly acquired courage, he approached an unattached young lady and asked her to dance. She accepted. They danced together several times. It was a great night, a wonderful night, this was *life*, such as he'd never known before. Tony looked forward all the next week to Saturday night, and the gaily lighted ballroom. He must ask his pal for another of those pills. He remembered he had been too excited to sleep that night, but he'd soon get over that.

Tony soon became a regular habitué of Birmingham's dance halls, with the pep pill as the inevitable prelude to the evening.

"I looked forward all week to Saturday night," he said, "but I just couldn't face it without the pills. I tried once, because I had to pay for them now, but I felt dreadful, and went home."

"And what then . . .?"

"One week my pal told me that he hadn't any pills, but he'd got something a lot better. He took me into the toilet and told me to roll up my sleeve . . . it hurt at first . . . but I felt great afterwards. It started then."

His voice trailed off to a whisper.

"In three weeks I was hooked on heroin, good and proper," he continued. "I managed to conceal it from my parents at first, but it was taking all my money, and I was using all sorts of excuses to get more. I started selling some of my stuff. I was missing out on my rugger and swimming, and I was getting irritable and bad-tempered. Poor Mum couldn't understand it. She could see the change in me, and kept asking me what was wrong."

He paused to wipe the perspiration from his face. Withdrawal had weakened him, and it seemed an effort to talk. I placed a reassuring hand on his.

"I suppose it all had to come out," Tony went on. "One night I hadn't been able to get my fix. I'd got no more money, and my Dad had got fed up with my demands. I don't blame him. I went to my room, and things got worse. At two o'clock in the morning it was nearly driving me bonkers. I suppose I started screaming. Dad and Mum came in to me. They were scared, and they sent for a doctor. I had to tell him. He gave me something to quieten me, and he arranged for me to come here."

I suggested to Tony that he should go to the farm with which I was involved, but his people were staunch Catholics, and we were evangelical Protestants, and Tony himself did not seem enthusiastic. He said that his people had arranged for him to go to relatives some distance from Birmingham, and after his discharge I did not hear of him for three months. I had asked him to keep in touch, and he said he would, but I did not have any word from him. I could only hope and pray.

Some time later, on one of my visits to the ward, the charge nurse told me that one of the patients had been asking for me. I went to a bed at the far end of the ward which he had indicated. It was Tony. He was very pale and emaciated and his black hair lay in long strands on the pillow. I spoke to him, but he was unresponsive, and it was some days before I could get him to tell me what had happened. He said he had stayed with a married sister in Leicester, and had kept clear for about two months. His parents assumed that his cure was final, and he had returned home.

"I just couldn't face it," he said, almost despairingly.

He seemed apathetic and remote. I was beginning to understand a little of the compelling sub-conscious urge of the drug-addict and the alcoholic, which supersedes and defies reason. It is more devastating than the physical addiction, and drives the victim to the limit of endurance, and yet he insistently clamours for more.

"I'd die for heroin," one young fellow had told me, and this was not the exaggeration of a sensation-seeking youth. It was the plain truth, wrung from a tortured soul. The hospital staff, with their understanding and patient nursing, could bring them through the worst pangs of withdrawal, and build up their much-abused bodies, but they just could not remedy the soul-sickness which persisted after their discharge. They came back, again and again and again, until the final failure and collapse.

I watched the frail, pallid youth on the bed. He was fumbling under the pillow.

"What are you looking for, Tony?" I asked gently.

"You wouldn't know," he answered. I knew he was a little bemused, and was searching for his syringe. I talked to him for some time, and he seemed a little calmer.

"Will you come and see me tomorrow?" he begged. I assured him that I would. "I'll be round early," I promised. I was very distressed at his state.

The following morning I made an unusually early visit, and I at once went over to his bed. It was empty.

"Where's Tony?" I asked the nurse.

"He died early this morning."

I felt shattered and disheartened. Could I have done more? Should I have exerted more pressure to induce him to join us on the farm? What was the answer to this critical period after hospitalisation? It was not an isolated case. It was happening too often. This, however, was the first time I had seen the sinister end, the final curtain on the tragedy. I felt bitterness in my heart towards those responsible for his first faltering steps, but as is so often the case, I knew that they were youngsters already themselves in the grip of the disease. I felt so utterly impotent and inadequate. They told me that Tony's case was exceptional, that of four million adolescents in the land, only eight hundred were heroin addicts. Statistics . . .? But Tony was not a statistic, he had been a living vibrant personality, loving and well-loved; until so recently a happy care-free youngster. Now he was limp and lifeless, on a cold slab!

I remembered that there were others in the ward. I remembered that we had an Almighty God who had the answer, even at the gate of eternity. Someone must tell them.

I was deeply shocked by Tony's death, but it made me more determined to continue, not in my own strength, but with simple faith in the One who had touched and healed the lepers.

A friend of mine was concerned at the time I spent in the ward.

"Why do you waste so much time on these folk?" he demanded, "when there are so many far more needy people? What about all the cripples, and the blind, and mentally handicapped, and yet you throw away your sympathy on those who are there entirely through their own fault? If they want to destroy themselves, why not let them?"

I have heard the same sentiments expressed many times, yet so often we have found that the first steps were taken either in innocence or ignorance. Most of us have, at some time, succumbed to temptation, and have repented and found restoration. The tragedy of drug-addiction is that repentance is so often too late for restoration.

I had known Nick for some time before he told me his story. He was a young man of unprepossessing appearance, with long blond hair, unshaven, unkempt, and often dirty. He seemed grateful for my interest, but was rather inarticulate. He was not reticent, but just unable to express himself in conversation. He was friendly with Roger, who also had been on heroin – an intelligent lad and the dominant personality in the friendship. It was from Roger that I learnt of Nick's early life. His father was a drunkard, and his mother had died while he was still in his early boyhood. Nick had known little of parental care and affection, and had often suffered physical violence from his father. He was mentally retarded, and after an unhappy childhood had found himself quite unable to cope with the demands of life. He had drifted into the sub-strata of society, and found that he was accepted and tolerated, and he fell an easy prey to the junkie fraternity. He was soon enslaved by drugs, and entered the twilight life of the addict, who knows no horizon beyond his next "fix", whose world alternates between the euphoria and fantasy of the drug, and the sheer misery and physical pain of withdrawal. Roger was a good-hearted lad, and he took Nick under his wing. He came to the hospital when life had become unsupportable, when the drug had lost its first potency, and the need for relief had become too urgent. Both lads became regular visitors to my house during their stay in hospital. It was Roger who came to me with an unusual request.

"When are you going to get your hair cut again?" he asked. I was taken aback by his question. I knew my visit was about due, but did not think it was that obvious.

"Probably tomorrow," I replied, "but why?"

"Can we come with you?" He seemed amused at my astonishment.

I knew I had never passed any derogatory remarks about their rather lavish hirsute adornments, nor did I ever criticise their appearance or dress style.

"Of course you can come, if you'd like to," I replied rather weakly. We had an easy relationship and I suspected a little leg-pulling."

On the following day I called at the usual time, and found to my surprise that they were both waiting. They clambered into my car, and off we went. They followed me into the chairs, and to my amazement asked for a "short back and sides". Two well-shorn young men accompanied me back to the wards, causing a minor sensation amongst the hospital staff. I was still rather baffled.

"What made you do it?" I asked them. It was always Roger who was the spokesman.

"You made us," he replied.

"Made you?"

"Well, we thought you'd like it," said Roger.

He was always self-possessed, but Nick had a rather sheepish grin. I was deeply moved, and for a while was bereft of words, but I think they both knew the depth of feeling behind my murmured thanks. On the following Sunday they came with me to the evening service at my church, and they both responded to an appeal at the end. How sincere was their commitment I shall never know. I arranged for both to be transferred to the farm on their discharge from the hospital, but neither stayed long. Roger never returned to his former life, and now has a wife and family, and a good job. Nick decided to return home in spite of my protests. I went to see him, and he was very wretched.

"I had a dream last night," he told me. "I dreamt that you were my father. I was so disappointed when I woke." The stubble had reappeared on his face, and the hair was straggling down, blond and dirty. He knew that once again he was rejected and unwanted. I promised to find him a "pad" (his jargon for a place to live), but when I returned a few days later he had gone. I learned that he had made his way to London, and shortly afterwards had died from an overdose of drugs. "I will have mercy on whom I will have mercy," said the Lord (Rom. 9:15). I sincerely believe that in his final hours Nick "looked and lived", like the dying thief. Poor, forgotten, dirty, alone. Christ died for such as he, and He did not die in vain.

To the uninitiated it is hard to comprehend the potency of some of the "hard" drugs, and their desolating impact on the human mind. Looking back on the trail of devastation I saw during the two years I spent among these people I could not but be appalled at the indifference to death. Youths in their teens, and young men in the prime of manhood, accept with apparent equanimity and unconcern an awareness that they are on a one-way ticket to the grave. You try to tell them, and they shrug their shoulders, and seem to regard you with a patronising air of tolerance. At times they will make abortive efforts to break the chains, but you sense their conviction that they will come back, that they are only seeking a temporary release.

Chris was a regular patient at the hospital unit. He was an intelligent young man, and fully aware of the implications of his addiction, and had often been through withdrawal. Within weeks he would be back, clamouring for his daily allowance of the drug, issued by the hospital to defeat the "black market", and to exercise some sort of control. In his worst moments, he would ask me to pray for him, and on one occasion he accompanied me to my church, although he was a professing Catholic. He expressed surprise that we worshipped "without any artificial aids". He appeared to know little about his own professed faith.

"I said 'The Lord's Prayer' twenty times for you last night," he told me one morning. I thanked him, but tried to explain the futility of "vain repetitions". He would always listen attentively to all I had to say, and we had many a long chat. He knew his health was deteriorating, and I asked him if he would join us on the farm.

"Give me another two weeks," he said, "and I'll come."

I think he meant it. He was living alone in a single room, in a seedy back street in Winson Green. He had taken a "fix" of heroin, and had fallen asleep with a lighted cigarette in his hand. It had ignited the settee, and he had been asphyxiated by smoke. They found his charred body amongst the debris some hours later.

Mick was a likeable lad, twenty years old, courteous and kind to all. How he had become originally involved I shall never know. He had had a good education, and had a good family background. He was given every encouragement by his people, and they had willingly consented to his hospitalisation, and a period on the farm. He spent odd days with us, but would never talk about his addiction, except to say that he had no further intention of going back to drugs. I had the impression, however, that he had lost interest in life. He was an easy-going chap, and there seemed little sign of motivation to re-establish himself. Try as we would, we never seemed to be able to penetrate the barriers of reserve. We were very sorry to hear he had left the farm without leaving us his address.

Within three weeks we heard he had died from an overdose of drugs.

And then there was Archie, a would-be tough gangster with too soft a heart, who dreamt of hair-raising exploits in the underworld, and who usually ended his exploits ignominiously in the cells of the local "lock-up". He was eighteen when I first met him. He looked rather wild and dishevelled with an unruly mop of hair, a pallid skin and an unshaven chin. He had already been a "heroin-driller" for over a year, and his appearance confirmed it. Poor Archie, he so wanted to be the "big-time guy", and yet was so naive and childlike, a big overgrown schoolboy. Sadly, the drug had supplied him with his dreams of grandeur, and inflated his ego. They were a refuge from the haunting reality of his own ineffective and inadequate self. We kept in touch over a period of twelve years. Three times I spoke for him in Court, on mitigation pleas. Again and again I visited him in prison in various parts of the country, even travelling as far as Dartmoor, where he served a three-year sentence. He had married, and over the years his attractive wife had been very loyal, struggling almost single-handed to keep a home together for him. He had two sons by the marriage, and the last arrival was christened Trevor Francis after the well-known footballer, who was then with Birmingham City. Archie was an enthusiastic supporter of the team.

He was thirty years old on his last visit to me. His wife had left him, but he did not reproach her. His old bravado had gone and he was broken and defeated. He asked me to pray for him, and we both knelt together in my sitting room. As I prayed Archie wept bitterly. We both felt very near to the One who had died for us. He promised to come again but he never did. He died some days later. The heart finally gave way under the strain of years of drugs and privations. I know that the time I spent with him was not in vain, and we shall meet again.

One is never immune to the heartache of these sad and sordid stories. Each one has its own poignancy when you know the real and living person behind the artificiality of their lives. Our Lord's heart of compassion reached out to all the ten lepers, but only one returned to give thanks and share the real blessing. There is a note of ineffable sadness in His question, "Where are the nine?"

We had an anxious enquiry from a Christian lady in Liverpool, whose son had become involved with drugs. He was living at home, and we arranged to call and see him. He was a tall fair-haired young man of twenty, and he received us well, with no apparent resentment. After a long chat on general topics, he was rather cynical when I broached the real purpose of our visit. Oddly enough, he seemed to welcome it when I suggested that we should call again. I enlisted the support of two young men from the Salem Church where my wife and I had been brought to the Lord, and between us we managed to form an association which lasted about two years. A great deal of prayer was offered up on his behalf, and our efforts were very persistent. It all seemed to no avail. One learns to be patient with these people, but I was becoming rather disheartened with our efforts. I called early one evening. He had gone to bed well doped with drugs. His mother was in great distress, and seemed to be giving up hope.

"He's in bed," she said, with an air of resignation. "You can see him if you want, but I don't think it's any use."

I went to his room. He was confused and incoherent. I uttered a silent prayer, and spoke to him about the power of Christ to deliver him. He showed no apparent response, and I left him. It seemed indeed a hopeless case. I tried to speak a few words of comfort to his mother, but I came away with the conviction that we were wasting our time. I was particularly distressed and disappointed on account of the two young men who with their church had so faithfully laboured and prayed.

"All we can do now is pray," I told them, not too convincingly I felt, but they had the resilience of youth, and they actually encouraged me. I was very concerned for the mother, who for so long had borne with her son's ill-temper during periods of depression which cloud the life of the addict, and who watched his gradual deterioration. Was the work in vain? Were the tears unheeded and the prayers unanswered?

The answer came in a letter I received some few weeks later. It is one of my most cherished possessions.

"Dear Mr Moore," it ran, "I would like to thank you for all your prayers. I know that you will be overjoyed to hear that they have been answered. I have come to know the Lord, and I'm now trusting in Him. I have so much to tell you, but I'd rather wait until I see you . . . May God bless you, Gary." This was soon followed by another letter.

"Thank you for your letters, and your prayers, which I know have been, and are, a great help. I was baptised on September 7 at our Baptist Church. It was a wonderful experience. I am a new person, and I know the road to peace and truth, which is Jesus. I also gave up smoking on September 7."

I asked later at what point he made his decision. He spoke of the talks he had had with the two young men, and their influence on his thinking, but he said the real crisis came on the evening when I spoke to him while he was actually under the influence of the drug. At what would seem the most hopeless and impossible moment, a light dawned on his "Damascus Road". In apparent defeat, there was a victory. We may not know how and when God answers prayer, but we learn to leave it in his hands.

That is five years ago, and Gary is now married to a Christian girl, and already has a small family, a house and a job. I shall always remember his words as he gave his testimony.

"It is wonderful to be delivered from drugs," he said, "but the real wonder, is the wonder of my salvation."

CHAPTER FIVE

FROM NEWHAVEN TO ADULLAM

Discipline at Hill Farm, set in the undulating Worcestershire countryside, was very strict. None of the men were allowed out without an escort, except by permission. There was a strict "No smoking" rule, which most of them found very irksome, and hard to accept. Several of the lads absconded, and inevitably drifted back to their former habits. It was discouraging and frustrating to see our efforts fading into futility. It would seem logical, and an acceptable theory, that every obstacle should be placed in the way of their obtaining drugs or alcohol. The committee was a group of sincere men, with strong religious convictions, and they were adamant in their opposition to any amelioration of the conditions. I had always insisted, however, that any rehabilitation must be supplemented by the consent and co-operation of the person concerned. It is a basic tenet of our faith that we have free will to choose for good or evil. If the addict or the alcoholic earnestly desires to free himself (or herself) from the slavery of their habit, we can help. If not, then deprivation only increases their determination to continue.

Let us be abundantly clear on this point. I do not advocate "kid-glove" treatment in our prisons and borstals.

Punishment should follow crime as surely as night follows day, and the severity of the punishment should be commensurable with the crime. The law must be impartial and inexorable. There should be an emphatic and clearly-defined line of demarcation between punishment and rehabilitation, and it is the lack of this that has caused the present-day confusion in the mind of the offender. There are persistent pressures from many well-intentioned but misguided people to eliminate the punitive element from our prisons and borstals, and substitute a structured but easy-going environment, where the offender may be coaxed to a better way of life. They are encouraged to believe that what they did was not so bad after all, and that society was not too concerned about it. On discharge, the homeless ones are provided with a home or institution, with a well-organised plan of behaviour, and a set of rules which are easily broken and defied when you are asked to conform, but where it does not matter very much if you don't. The young folk, so often brought up to a contempt of the law, are understandably confused. The older ones are cynical. A sentence of imprisonment is regarded as an acceptable hazard, tolerable, and just a temporary curtailment of their way of life. The imposition of shorter, sharper sentences, with the rigorous discipline of the old army "glasshouse" but without its harsh brutality, would greatly enhance our chances of effective rehabilitation, and ease some of the intolerable pressure on our prison system. Crime would no longer be regarded as a profitable enterprise, with minimal risks. Having paid the price, however, we as Christians should see to it that we offer a more attractive way of life, and warm-hearted companionship. Let them be brought into our society, and into our homes, not with tolerance, or on sufferance, but as "brethren beloved", and fellow-citizens.

I would have preferred more freedom on the farm. Dan and Norma Wooding, a young couple, were the first Wardens. What they lacked in experience, was more than made up for by their enthusiasm and dedication. They had a friendly, easy-going approach, and usually there was a happy relationship with the men. It was inevitable, however, that tensions at times were high. We were dealing with volatile temperaments, and with surges of resentment and rebellion against the restrictions. Dan and Norma needed periods of rest and recuperation, which with our limited resources we were unable to give. To be isolated day-after-day, and week-after-week, in such an environment, and under such pressures, finally brought them to the verge of a breakdown, and they were compelled to leave. My association with Dan and Norma had brought to me, however, a wealth of understanding of the problems involved, and a clearer insight into the mind of the addict. It was a sad day for all concerned when the young couple left the farm. They were followed by an elderly couple, who continued bravely for some months, but who finally had to give in under the strain.

There was an urgent need for the farm. The hospitals were doing a splendid job in bringing the addicts through the stages of withdrawal under qualified supervision, but obviously they could not hope to provide the essential aftermath of rehabilitation. We had made many additions and improvements to the farm premises, and the building had been done economically, by voluntary labour. The amenities were generally good, and the food was ample. There was a high standard of comfort and cleanliness throughout. It would seem that we had the solution to our difficulty, but we did not appear to achieve the results for which we hoped. There were too many apparent failures, and too much disruption and unrest. The committee was concerned, but my suggestions were not well-received. I told them I would have preferred rather less rigidity in the rules, and less restriction in movement. These sentiments may have helped, I do not know, but from henceforward I seemed to be regarded as a subversive element, and after a committee meeting which I had been unable to attend, I received a brief letter to say that they had unanimously decided to ask me to resign. It was a bitter blow. It had seemed a great venture, a real step of faith, and I had given it so much of my time and substance. The farm seemed to be essentially complementary to the work in the drug-addiction unit at All Saints Hospital. I was now a lifeboat-man without a lifeboat, a shepherd without a pasture for the sheep. I had yet to learn "All things work together for good . . .", and that I was the sheep, being guided and diverted by the crook of the Good Shepherd. "I'll bless the hand that guided, I'll bless the heart that planned." I decided to align myself with the Birmingham branch of "Christian Action" under the chairmanship of Archdeacon Vernon Nicholls, now the Bishop of Sodor and Man. The branch was mainly concerned with the vagrancy problem, and the alleviation of destitution. We managed to provide a night shelter in the Crypt of St. Chad's, Birmingham's Cathedral, which met an immediate and urgent need, but I had nothing to offer the men who were now my main concern, people like Nick, and Archie, and so many more. We wanted something to replace the "pad", the very sub-standard and often revolting accommodation to which they had been reduced. A home and the security of a fire-side was the first pre-requisite in the fight for a new and better life. We made several abortive enquiries, but nothing seemed to materialise.

It was then that we had the amazing sequence of events which brought Newhaven into being. A young university student, who had for some time been a voluntary helper with the organisation, told me of a private hotel in squalid Balsall Heath which was for sale at a very low price. It had been used by a charitable organisation for accommodating homeless people, and they were anxious to dispose of it. They could only offer it on a short lease of about two or three years, but the cost was low, and I saw its potential. The hotel was offered to "Christian Action", and they agreed to take it over. An Anglican brotherhood volunteered to take on the management, but they insisted that the premises should be vacated by all the existing tenants, to enable them to start from scratch. There were three rooms occupied by immigrant families, and short of applying for eviction orders, which they obviously would not do, there was little hope of immediate action. I had already assured the vendor of our intention to purchase, and I completed the deal. I was now the sole owner of a seventeen-roomed hotel, only partially furnished, and urgently requiring a coat of paint. It was in one of the more disreputable districts of the city, a notorious red light area. I had no staff, and after my investment in Hill Farm, my own funds were rather low. My colleagues on the Committee were critical of my action. I was nearly seventy years of age, with its inevitable toll of strength, and I knew I could not cope, alone. It was then I stood back, and saw God move.

It all happened so quickly. Paint and emulsion were supplied from one source, and a group of volunteers from Birmingham University provided the labour. Furniture arrived, and then sheets and bedding, and then came leather-faced, old Jack, to somehow meet all of our staff requirements, competent, enthusiastic, and unpaid. Newhaven was a going concern. I had learned to "stand still, and see the salvation of the Lord" (Exodus 14:13).

We had one large room set aside for worship, and Dan Wooding's father, the Rev. Alfred Wooding, then pastor of the Sparkbrook Mission, came along to take the dedication service. It was a very moving occasion. We held a service every Sunday evening for the next two years. There was no hint of compulsion, but I never knew an occasion when at least two or three men did not attend, and the room was often full. Contact was made with the Welfare Service at Winson Green Prison, and we offered to provide accommodation for homeless discharged prisoners.

We were extending our horizons, and it was not long before all our rooms were occupied. There was a communal dining-room and lounge, but each man had his own room, to which he could retire at any time, if he so wished. There was complete freedom of action, and no restrictive rules. It was understood that there must be no liquor brought into the premises, and they must not invite their girlfriends into their own rooms. This was explained to them on arrival, not as a rule, but as a code of honour. There was seldom an infringement of the former, and to the best of my knowledge, never of the latter. This freedom was usually appreciated, and seldom imposed upon. It restored their dignity and self-respect, and provided the basis of a mutual understanding and confidence. Friendships were established which have lasted through the years, and will last through eternity.

The men came from all walks of life, many with long records of criminal activity and violence. We did not enquire into their background, but they often talked to us, and we so often found that they were just ordinary folk like ourselves, with the same emotions, and the same aspirations. There was usually a history of a broken home, and a childhood devoid of discipline or instruction in any code of ethics.

A few extra hours booked on the timesheet, a fictitious expense account, and "accidental" omission from a tax return are fairly safe acceptable ways of theft from the individual or the community. If you're found out, there is little more than a shrug of the shoulders, or an amused tolerance. These people, however, have been prepared to recognise the risks involved and to accept the challenge. They declare open war on society, and make a direct frontal attack. The tax dodger and the timesheet fiddler are a fifth column with an almost impenetrable cloak of respectability. The objectives are identical, and the end-product is the same.

Newhaven survived for two-and-a-half years. Through it we made our first contact with the Probation Service, the beginning of a long and rewarding association with so many officers of sterling quality and ability. They gave us great encouragement, and every assistance, although some were a little dubious about our methods. They were also able to obtain for us some financial help from the Home Office, easing the intense pressure on our meagre resources. Any misgivings or apprehensions they may have had about our ability to control our people quickly disappeared. The local police did not appear to know that we existed. We had many persistent offenders, but to the best of my knowledge there were no charges against any of our men during their stay with us. Towards the end, old Jack's health was failing. He fought with tremendous courage an incipient disease, which we found to be terminal cancer and we finally procured for him a small self-contained flat. A few months later he was removed to hospital, where he died three months afterwards. Although he had a formidable record of crime and violence, we owed him a great debt. He had his own standards of integrity, and he was always intensely loyal. It grieved him to know that Newhaven was to be demolished, as a prelude to a big road widening scheme, and it hastened his end.

He had been proud of what we had accomplished, and somehow felt that what he had done was a belated effort to repay his debt to society, and to establish himself as an honest citizen. At the end he had a sincere and simple faith in God.

We managed to acquire three more houses in the area, in an attempt to perpetuate the work we had begun. We formed ourselves into a housing association with the inevitable committee, but the members disagreed on the choice of a successor to Jack. I wanted a man from the ranks of the residents, who had known the privations of life behind prison walls. My colleagues sought a man with more academic qualifications, and a better social background. Once again I found myself alone in opposition. To avoid further friction, I decided to resign. This, I felt, was surely the end. I was now seventy-two and again discarded. I do not offer any criticism of the attitude of the committee. They pinned their faith on traditional practice, and were sincere in their convictions. I appreciated the risk attached to my unorthodox methods. They had proved successful during the regime of old Jack, but then he was an exceptional man, and it would seem logical and acceptable to revert to well-established procedure. A well-disciplined and structured environment would be the pattern for the future Newhaven.

I found to my surprise that I was not quite alone. Three men from old Newhaven cornered me, and said that if I would continue they would offer their services free if necessary. I explained to them the difficulty of acquiring suitable accommodation, and the costs involved. They were sympathetic but insistent. I did not want to disappoint them. We talked it over, and I said that if it was God's will, the way would open. The next day I passed a small terraced house in Handsworth on the north side of Birmingham which had a notice "For sale by auction". I asked the three men to come with me to inspect it, and we obtained the key from the agents. It seemed ideally suitable for us. I did not know a great deal about valuation of property, but I knew the limit of my resources. It appeared the previous owner had paid £1,760 for it, and was anxious to at least recuperate the price. I said I would go to the auction and bid up to £1,500. If it went beyond that figure I would understand that it was not God's will for us to continue. All three men, Fred, Bob and John, turned up at the auction. The bidding started at £750, and climbed slowly by £25 bids. £1,400 . . . £1,450 . . . £1,475 . . . I once more raised my finger . . . £1,500 . . . Silence . . . going at £1,500 . . . the hammer descended. "Adullam Homes" was born.

We needed furnishings, cutlery, curtains, and many alterations, but I knew now that every need would be met. This would be our pilot scheme, a blueprint for future development. It would be a home where men would be able to live with a minimum of supervision and the maximum of freedom. It would not be a hotel, or boarding-house, or hostel but HOME in the true sense of the word. It would provide the essential basis for the structure of a new life.

Within a few months we had the offer of a further house at a very low price, and yet a third was provided for us, through his Trust, by Mr Brandon Cadbury, a member of the famous chocolate factory. This was a great encouragement, and a confirmation of our step of faith. There were one or two setbacks, all the houses needed bathrooms, and plans were duly prepared and accepted by the City Council as eligible for a fifty per cent grant. Work was put in hand on two of them, but then to our dismay the City now refused payment on the ground that the houses were "multi-occupied". We only had three men to a house, each with a bedroom of his own, but this did not appear to satisfy the bureaucratic mind, and therefore we had to pay the whole cost. It appeared that if you house a family of ten in a small terraced house it is acceptable, but if you house three men in the same house it is "multi-occupied", and incurs the disapproval of the City Fathers. We had much to learn in these early days, and owe a great debt of gratitude to a local architect, Mr Jim Coton, who had shown a concern for our work. He guided us through the many pitfalls of house purchase and improvement, and put in a tremendous amount of voluntary work which finally enabled us to form a housing association of our own. It opened the door to the acquisition of further properties, and by 1975 we had ten houses and about thirty residents. Some supervision was of course always needed, but we found that the ratio of staff to residents was adequate at 1:15, whereas the average ratio in most hostels for ex-offenders was in the region of 1:2½ or 1:3. This was an attractive economy if our methods proved successful. Our initial costs in furnishings were also very modest, as so much was given to us in gifts from so many sources.

The local probation service was ever at our elbow, with support and encouragement, and the majority of residents were channelled through their service, although a few were sent by Prison Welfare. Their officers knew and understood our methods, and the men were selected on their adaptability and motivation. No man was excluded on account of his record, however extensive or sinister. The first offender or the recidivist were equally welcome, but we always looked for a sincere desire to start afresh. Even a tiny spark of motivation could be fanned into a flame in the right environment. It is inevitable that we made mistakes. A probation officer from another office phoned us to ask if we would accept a married couple. The man had a bad record including a case of "grievous bodily harm", and the woman was an alcoholic. I had not been supplied with a report, and knew little of their background. Although we did not usually receive a married couple, I agreed to interview them, and they arrived on a Saturday morning. They told me a sad tale of being thrown out by a heartless landlord, and said that they had no means and nowhere to go. The woman was about forty and was older than the man. I said I would provide them with temporary accommodation, if they would do their utmost to find a place of their own. As it was at the weekend I could not contact the probation officer involved, and the need was immediate. They were both living on Social Security support and had apparently already spent their week's allowance.

We soon had cause to regret our hospitality. There was continuous quarrelling, and they proved to be a disruptive influence in the home. We were concerned also for another young couple living in the same house, and who had a small child. They were having to endure a nightly ordeal of brawling and debauchery. Having settled in, Tom and his wife showed no inclination to move, and all our efforts to get them alternative accommodation were met with sullen defiance. Their payments were spasmodic and they were soon in arrears. They were also associating with another man, an alcoholic, who had a long record of crime. As a home for ex-offenders, we were anxious to preserve our anonymity, and maintain good relations with our neighbours, but Tom and his wife were becoming a little too well-known. Complaints were made by the other residents that the home was beginning to receive some notoriety. Finally we told them they must go, but they tried to take refuge in the Rent Act. We knew the difficulty this would present, and the lengthy process in the Courts to secure an Eviction Order.

The couple had now become aggressively hostile, and visited my local church while under the influence of drink, and attempted to disrupt the service. The minister handled the situation with consummate tact, but it was the precursor of many more irritations and embarrassments, and the situation steadily deteriorated.

The crisis came one night at about 9.30 p.m. I had a telephone call from the young couple who were sharing the house. The husband said that Tom and his wife and the other man were all in their bedroom, very drunk, and causing annoyance to the whole neighbourhood. It was followed shortly afterwards by another call from a nearby house, threatening to summon the police if we did not take immediate action. I telephoned the home of a friend in the Probation Service. He was sympathetic, and said he would contact the local police, and ask them to deal with the matter. A police-car was despatched to the house, but the Superintendent phoned me just before midnight to say that they were unable to intervene, as no law had been broken and the other man had been invited into the house by the occupants. He was very understanding, but explained that his hands were tied unless there had been a breach of the peace. It was an impossible situation, and could have a severe impact on our credibility, apart from any moral implications. We who believe in God, however, have always an answer to man's helplessness. When we have reached the ultimate in our own puny efforts, when we have hurled our all against the barrier ahead, and we fall back, bruised and broken, and utterly defeated, there is the almost involuntary cry to our Creator.

I knew that only Divine intervention could help. I fell on my knees in my room.

"Lord," I cried, "it cannot be Your will that this situation should continue, deliver us from this evil. Thou art the God of the impossible."

I felt an immediate reassurance. I had handed my burden over to the Master, and we retired to rest, conscious that it was entirely in His hands. I was in my office at 8.30 a.m. on the following morning, and after a few minutes the telephone rang. I recognised the voice of Charles, the other tenant.

"Is that you, Mr Moore?"

"Yes, Charles, what is happening?"

"Tom is dead . . ."

He waited several seconds for my reaction, and then told me briefly what had happened. Tom's wife had been the first to awake. She had staggered to her feet, and had discovered her husband on the bed, his face a bluish colour, and showing no sign of life. She managed to awaken the other man, and they both tried to rouse Tom, without success. Realising he was dead, the man fled, and was not seen again. The wife, distraught and dishevelled, rushed round to my house, but we did not hear the bell, and she went to the Police Station. An ambulance was summoned, but all efforts to revive Tom failed.

We did what we could for the stricken wife, attended the inquest with her, and arranged for the funeral, but she left us to seek the comfort of some friends, and we did not see her again.

The inquest verdict was one of suicide. From the rather disjointed and incoherent accounts, however, it appeared that he must have swallowed a number of barbiturate tablets while under the influence of drink. I saw his cold stiff body in the mortuary. They had dyed his prematurely grey hair black. He looked pathetically young, and I felt a great surge of pity for his wasted life. I have tried to record the circumstances factually and impartially. We have a merciful but an omnipotent and omniscient God.

CHAPTER SIX

"AH'VE NAE WHERE TAE GO"

It was Jock who gave me my first and greatest lesson in dealing with the alcoholic. As his nickname implies, he was a little Scotsman, sharp-featured, and with a very pronounced accent. He was a native of Aberdeen, and about fifty years old, but in spite of many years of heavy drinking, he was still active, and youthful-looking. I first met him in the drug-addiction unit at All Saints Hospital. We soon became good friends, and he was a regular visitor at my home. When sober, he was a loyal husband, and a devoted father, but his compulsive drinking had relentlessly ruined his family life, estranged his friends, and left him a lonely man. His was a sad story. Week after week, his wages had all gone on whisky, and then he resorted to selling any item of value, first his own, and then those of his wife, and finally the last degrading act, taking the savings of his own children. His wife had borne it all with love and forbearance, hope restored by periods of penitence, and then dashed and destroyed by further bouts of drunkenness, ending in mute despair.

It had to end. She told him he must go, and this time his pleading was in vain. He left, but always cherishing the hope of reconciliation, until the final decree of dissolution. Jock loved his wife and children, but he was hopelessly enslaved to his addiction. He had already been in three hospitals when we met, and was not too optimistic about his future and his ultimate chances of recovery. He had tried so many times and failed.

I took him along to my local evangelical church. Jock responded well to the ministry, and at the end of one evening service made a real commitment to Christ. He joined us in our prayers, and attended all the meetings which were held in our large "upper room" every evening. Some four months elapsed, and he had not touched a drop of liquor. He had been trained as a male nurse, and he had the offer of a job in a geriatric ward at a local hospital. Beneath his fairly cheerful exterior, however, I sensed a deep longing for his family. He was basically and essentially a family man. His eldest son was serving with the Forces in India and he wrote him a long and pathetic letter, telling him of his new resolution, and his new life, and of his remorse for the past. He pleaded for him to write to him. We could not but notice the increased depression as no letter arrived in response. Weeks went by, and then it came. It was not from his son, but a curt note from his commanding officer to say that the lad did not wish to have any further communication with his father. Before we could reach him Jock was hopelessly drunk.

We tried to help. On five occasions I took him back to the hospital in an advanced stage of inebriation, often trying to resist our help. He was penitent after each outburst, but as soon as he could get money he was back in the pub, and we seldom knew which one. It is so easy to adopt a pharisaical attitude of condemnation, and say "Enough.

We've done our best for you. It's your own choice. If you want to go to your ruin, then *go*." One day I found him in my home, maudlin and incoherent, and very drunk. For the first time, I told him to go, and had to partially assist him to the door. I shall never forget his rather bemused but pathetic expression as I shut the door.

"Ah've nae where tae go," he said. I did not recognise the despair. I never saw Jock again, and was never able to trace him. We've prayed for him long and earnestly over the years, but I learned the meaning of the words of our Lord to Peter, telling him to forgive "seventy times seven" if need be. I had learned this lesson when I first met Paddy.

I was paying one of my now less frequent visits to the drug-addiction and alcoholic unit at All Saints Hospital. One of the young men I knew asked me if I would have a word with an older man on the other side of the ward.

"'E reckons 'e's goin' to do 'imself in," he told me.

I was not unduly impressed. I had heard the words too often amongst these folk. They seldom carried out their threat. I went to the man's bedside, and spoke to him. He was slowly recovering from a severe bout of heavy drinking, and was in a mood of black depression. He told me a sorry tale of the misery he had brought to his home, his wife and his boy, a lad nine years old.

"I'm not fit to be a father," he said. His real concern seemed to be for his son. He was in his late forties, a fairly well built Irishman from Dublin. He had been brought up a Roman Catholic, but did not practise his religion. He was a very intelligent chap, and we had quite a long talk. I promised I would visit him again.

"Everybody calls me Paddy," he told me, when I asked for his name. He gave me his home address, and

I promised to see his wife and boy. The next time I visited, he seemed much better, and was making the usual resolutions for his future. He told me something of his early life. He had had his first drink at the age of sixteen. It seemed to him quite a normal and acceptable way of life, and he told me he saw the priest drinking in the bar. It boosted his ego to pay for a round of drinks. His father had also been a heavy drinker, and Paddy left home to join the Irish army at the age of seventeen, and then deserted and crossed the border to join the RAF in Ulster. In 1945, at the end of the Second World War, he was sent with the British Forces to Germany. Wine and lager were cheap in those days, and Paddy was very popular. There were boisterous evenings in the Biergartens, with heavy drinking. Slowly, surely and inexorably, his body built up a resistance and a dependence on alcohol. Tensions mounted, and he had increasing difficulty in coping with them. He found the only relief in yet more drinking, and as the tensions increased, so the need became ever more urgent. Paddy did not often get drunk, but he noticed that at the end of the evening the stress disappeared. He had reached the stage of "emotional anaesthesia". With this, came an increased tolerance, and an ever increasing capacity and insistence. He was in the "pre-alcoholic addiction" stage. The inevitable happened, and after several warnings he was at last found drunk on "Guard duty", a very serious offence. He was sentenced to a month in the "glasshouse", the army punishment barracks, so much feared in the forces. There is an iron discipline, and everything must be done "at the double". If you are given a command, you must run. There is no malingering, and no respite. It was a hard lesson, and Paddy had no desire to repeat the dose.

With such a threat hanging over his head, he managed to keep sober until his discharge.

Back in England, on completion of his service, Paddy came to Birmingham, and obtained work at a garage as a semi-skilled mechanic. He was competent and adaptable, and after learning to drive, obtained a Heavy Goods Vehicle Licence. He later obtained employment as a long-distance coach driver. In the meantime he got married, and after a while managed to get a home together. A son was born, and everything seemed to be "set fair". Relentlessly, however, the cancerous growth of alcoholism was extending its sinister grip. The social evenings in the pub became more and more frequent. An ever-increasing proportion of the week's wages was being consumed at the expense of the household purse. There was domestic discord and quarrelling, and as the tension in the home increased, the need became more urgent for escape from emotional stress. With the typically irrational alcoholic reasoning, he tended to put the blame on his wife. He realised, however, that he was now losing control of his drinking, and that after the first pint he lost the ability to stop until nature intervened with sickness, or complete intoxication. There were periods of remorse, but these only accentuated his need for more liquor. He was driving coaches, with the lives of passengers in his hands, and he was gravely aware of the terrible responsibility that was his. He consulted his doctor, and it was finally agreed that he should receive treatment, and after a further bout he was referred to All Saints, where I met him.

Within three weeks of his discharge, he was drinking again. He was now dependent upon alcohol for his driving, and knew that sooner or later there would be disaster if he continued. To his credit, he recognised the danger with all its implications, and he resigned his job. When sober he was an extremely competent driver, and he loved the work, but he chose to sacrifice his job and his livelihood rather than place others at risk. He managed to obtain a job at a factory, but the wages were poor, and insufficient to meet his ever-increasing demand for drink. He could no longer face the reproaches of his wife, and life at home became progressively worse.

Then came the night of climax. All his money was gone, and he was tortured by his intolerable craving for drink. He walked the streets until the pubs closed, and for what seemed an eternity afterwards. In the early hours of the morning he reached his home, and quietly entered. The house was silent. He fumbled his way to the kitchen. The cat was asleep on the hearth. The boy's shirts, recently ironed, were on the clothes-horse beside the fireplace. Everything in the room seemed to reproach him and pour out its scorn. Even the cat was aloof, utterly ignoring him. Very quietly he opened the door of the gas oven, placed a cushion inside, and lay down, his head on the cushion . . . and turned on all the taps. . . .

About 4 a.m. his wife, a light sleeper, noticed the smell of gas, and went downstairs.

The cat was dead, but Paddy's life hung on by a slender thread in the intensive-care unit of the hospital. Consciousness slowly returned after two weeks, but irreparable damage was done. He had difficulty in co-ordinating his thoughts, and in articulation, and was only a pale replica of his former self. No longer could he face the future and plan his life. There was just a numbed and passive acceptance of the present. His wife refused to have him back, and his son seemed estranged.

For over two long years he was incarcerated in the psychiatric wards of All Saints Hospital. Divorce proceedings were instituted, and for Paddy hope had gone. He mutely endured an existence among mentally retarded and inadequate people, unable to assume responsibility for himself, but yet acutely and painfully aware of his pitiful plight, with a mind alert to its misery and futility. It was the bleakest, darkest period of his life, and there seemed to be no road back. He became increasingly dependent on the protective environment of the hospital, and was in grave danger of becoming completely "institutionalised". I visited him fairly regularly, and offered him accommodation in our homes, as we gradually became established, and acquired more property. He at first refused all our offers, but then it seemed a real answer to our prayers when he suddenly decided to make the break. The doctor at the hospital was not optimistic about his chances, and seemed to indicate that his case was hopeless, but he made no objection to his discharge. Paddy came to one of our homes, but for some time he seemed nervous and tense, and although he knew it was contrary to our wishes, he again had recourse to bouts of drinking. There was little we could do. His divorce was now absolute and irrevocable, and any slender hopes he may have had of a reconciliation were finally dashed. Alcohol was his only escape from his remorse, and I was soon doubting the wisdom of the move. He was living with another man who had a long history of drink offences and Paddy's drinking was having an adverse effect on him. Unfortunately we had no alternative accommodation at the time.

It was Christmas Day, and my wife and I were just finishing our meal, on what we had hoped would be a quiet day, when the telephone rang. Would I come over at once, Paddy had come home drunk, and had upset the Christmas dinner all over the floor. I went round to the house, and found him in a truculent mood, and the other man in a state of exasperation. I knew that if he were pushed too far it would cause another breakdown, and a further outburst of heavy drinking. I felt that priority should be given to the one who was determinedly trying to keep sober. I asked Paddy to find other accommodation, at least temporarily, and he went. After a few nights in a cheap men's hostel, he was given a place in the new Newhaven. He stayed for a short period, until his continuous drinking and persistent state of intoxication became intolerable. He spent a night in the Crypt, a shelter for the destitute, and one or two nights in derelict houses. He was in great distress, and made yet another abortive attempt at oblivion, swallowing a quantity of barbiturate tablets. He was picked up in a semi-conscious condition by the police, and charged with being drunk and incapable, although he had actually had no liquor. He was penniless.

Paddy came back to us on the following day, in a very forlorn state. He had now indeed plumbed the depths, and in his despair, for the first time in his life, he sought Christ. He had been brought up a Roman Catholic, but had never known the real meaning of the Cross. In simple faith he committed his life to Christ. He was intensely moved by the words of the hymn:

> In tenderness he sought me,
>   Weary and sick with sin,
>   and on his shoulders brought me,
>   Back to the fold again.

Paddy realised that in his darkest hours, the hand of the Lord was over him, even through the "valley of the shadow of death". His recuperation has been slow, but very sure. His cigarettes followed his liquor into the limbo of forgotten things. He has been able to renew his driving licence, and now drives with confidence, free from the grim spectre of reflexes fuddled by drink.

We learn an understanding and a compassion for the drug-addict and the alcoholic. They are driven by a compulsion of the sub-conscious mind, over which they have little or no control. Apart from brief periods of euphoria, their life is one of misery and melancholy. Ostracised by society, and estranged from their nearest and dearest friends, often deprived of life's most elementary comforts, they drag on to what they know must be an early grave. They resist the would-be helper, and resist every effort made to save them from their mad helter-skelter to the pit.

Whatever the form of addiction, whether of drugs or alcohol, it must be recognised as a sickness of the mind, needing our care and concern, and causing as much or more distress to the patient as any recognised malady. Sometimes a resolute effort of will, a rigid determination of total abstinence, will achieve success, but with so many the powers of resistance have been gradually eroded. These are the people who need our help, and a persevering patience, when so often they receive our condemnation, our obvious irritation and final rejection. Jock was very sensitive to this, and probably felt that I had failed him. One can do little while they are actually under the influence of liquor, but I should have given him an assurance that he could return when sober. We do have some apparent failures in our homes, but they usually come back. They know that there is never a final rejection. There is an urgent need throughout the land for the under-standing and sympathetic helper, and a great opportunity for the Christian church. Sadly, we see most of them "pass by on the other side". They shrink away from contamina-tion, almost with revulsion, as they shrank from the leper in the days of our Lord. These people may be dirty, unkempt and objectionable, they may reek of stale beer and tobacco, poor gibbering travesties of humanity, but where now are those pioneer warriors like those of the early days of the Salvation Army, with their indomitable courage? The Army did not fear to enter the strongholds of their enemy, to drag the people from the pubs, and sometimes from the gutter. It is a sad reflection on our Christian church that so little is done to succour these poor sick folk. When we tell them of their plight, many will say "I'll pray for them". We believe in prayer, and we believe in miracles. They do happen, as we have so often proved, but where are today's Samaritans, who are prepared to step aside and dress the gaping wounds, to place the poor man on their own beast, and walk alongside, and to delve into their own resources to provide shelter and a restful bed? "Insomuch as ye did it unto one of these . . . ."

CHAPTER SEVEN

LIFE AND DEATH OF MOLLY

It was Saturday night, and I had made a routine call at the Christian Action reception centre near Birmingham's well-known Bull Ring. The rain had been pouring steadily down for some hours when the couple arrived. They were both drenched to the skin, utterly weary, dirty and bedraggled. The woman was in her early twenties, and the man was not much older. There was a look of mute appeal in her eyes. Her sodden, untidy hair trailed in wet strands over her face. The man said they had no money, and nowhere to go, and there was little chance of obtaining help from any of the usual channels at this late hour. We had no accommodation for married couples at Newhaven, but their need was urgent and immediate, and we felt we could not turn them out into the streets. I telephoned "old Jack", and he said he would get a room ready, and a hot bath. I took them over, and by the time we arrived Jack had already prepared a hot meal. Molly (that is not her real name) was pathetic in her gratitude, and seemed anxious to please. We managed to provide them both with dry clothing, and they were soon comfortably ensconced by a warm fire. The following day her "husband" left, on the pretext of looking for a job, and was never seen again. Little-by-little, and punctuated by bouts of weeping, Molly blurted out her story.

At a very early age, she had been rejected by her parents in Ireland, and had been brought up by a reluctant grandmother, who had regarded her as a burden on her rather meagre resources. The grandmother had arranged a marriage for Molly at the age of sixteen. At nineteen, Molly was the mother of two children, a boy and a girl, and tied to a husband who showed little or no affection for her. It was understandable that she had a distorted sense of moral values. She wanted to love and be loved, and almost inevitably became involved with an unscrupulous admirer. Her husband found out, and immediately put her out, and instituted divorce proceedings, upon which her "friend" abandoned her, and disappeared without trace. Cut off from all contact with her children, disowned by her husband, and rejected by her lover, she had a complete breakdown, and became partially paralysed. After a long period in hospital, she was discharged into a friendless and pitiless world, with no home and no means. Her story at this stage became rather incoherent and disjointed, and one felt that she was concealing the more sordid elements. Molly obviously lacked the sophistication and commercial acumen of a "woman of the streets", and her dire necessity had no doubt been exploited by unscrupulous men. She had neither physical stamina nor moral fibre and was bewildered by the cruel buffetings of life. Poor Molly. She begged me to write to the address where her two children were in a foster-home, and enquire about them. This we did, but received a very terse reply from the person in charge that they were both well, and had no wish for any further contact.

Newhaven was almost exclusively a male establishment, and Molly was becoming a rather embarrassing problem. She told us that she had a married sister in Birkenhead, and we at last managed to trace her. After an exchange of letters, the sister consented to give her a home for the time being. We arranged for Molly to go there, and after a while I visited her at her sister's home. She seemed to be integrated into the family, and appeared to be quite happy in her new environment. We were relieved to think that another human problem had been satisfactorily solved.

However, after about three months Molly returned. It seemed that her illness had left her with a rather distressing and embarrassing weakness, causing incontinence. Her sister's family had been rather intolerant, and had finally and abruptly told her to go. Molly appreciated our difficulty in again finding her accommodation, and it was she herself who again offered a solution. She said that she was sure that her grandmother would be glad for her to return, as the old lady was now alone. She lived in Belfast, where Molly had been brought up. I suggested that she wrote to her as a preliminary to her visit, but Molly insisted that she should go in person, and unheralded. We provided all she needed, and arranged for her to travel on the night boat from Heysham,

It had been a bad crossing, and Molly had been very sick. She felt limp and cold in the damp morning air at the quayside, and thought longingly of the homely comforts of her grandma's fireside. She made her way through the quayside offices with her one battered suitcase, and along the rather dismal streets until she came to the familiar door. She knocked with some trepidation. She waited awhile and knocked again. There was a shuffling from the interior, and the door was slowly opened, and a familiar face peered out.

"Hello, Gran," she said weakly.

"What are you doing here?" The old lady's voice was cold, and her expression hostile.

"Can't I come in?" begged Molly, feebly.

"Come in? You'll never cross this doorstep while I live. Never . . . never . . . you wicked woman . . ." The old woman almost spat the words. Molly stood in helpless misery, as the old lady poured out a torrent of invective and abuse, followed by a vicious and determined slam of the door.

Molly stood on the pavement, still holding her suitcase, put her hand on the wall for support.

"I've nowhere to go," she whispered. She was talking to herself, or maybe to the empty street.

We received a telephone call from the police in Belfast, and arrangements were made for her to return to Birmingham. For the time being we managed to get her into a local hostel, and finally found her a small flat.

Molly never recovered from the heartache of that last rejection. She asked very little of life. She had a warm heart which responded to any little kindness shown, and she had a simple childlike faith in God. We managed to furnish her material needs, and visited her as often as we could, but she was now eight miles away, and we had many other responsibilities which were equally demanding. It was just impossible to give her the daily companionship and caring she needed so much. Loneliness engulfed and overwhelmed her. She met an elderly man who sympathised with her. He was a widower of sixty-eight years, and as both were very lonely, this no doubt provided ground for mutual attraction. We were suddenly informed that they had decided to marry. There was little we could do. The man had no means of support beyond his old age pension, and Molly had no conception of domestic economy. They were an ill-assorted pair. The man's health was failing, and it was not long before he was confined to a wheelchair, and was later transferred to hospital suffering from a malignant tumour. She visited him every day, but he insisted on keeping control of his pension, and demanded that she brought it to him every week. He allowed her a pittance for housekeeping, which was invariably overspent by the end of the week. On one occasion she tried to augment it by a little flutter at the betting-shop. Sadly, as events proved, she won, and the following week, in desperate need of cash for clothing, she put the whole amount on what she had been assured was a "dead cert". As usual, the bookmaker won, and Molly felt she could not face her husband's fury. She had no friends, apart from ourselves, and for some reason she made no attempt to contact us. It is on such occasions that so many resort to crime. The sudden crisis, an overwhelming need to be met, and there will be the spontaneous reaction of the individual, conforming to the temperament, personality and conscience of the person concerned. Molly was frightened, but she had neither the will nor the courage to steal, or the initiative to seek help, and she had no one immediately available in whom to confide. Her problem could so easily have been dealt with, but in her loneliness it assumed gigantic proportions, and we shall never know the anguish of mind she endured, with no human companionship, and nobody who seemed to care.

The caretaker found her unconscious, slumped on the settee, a half-empty bottle of sleeping tablets at her side. They rushed her to hospital, and did all they could, but the brain was irreparably damaged, and she never roused from the coma. It was two days later when we first heard of the tragedy. My wife and I visited her, but we hardly recognised the Molly that we knew. She stared at us with unseeing eyes, a travesty of the girl we had known. On the last occasion we prayed at her bedside, and I thought I saw a flicker of recognition and a faint response. At that moment I believe that she joined us in a cry to the One who died for her on the cross. My wife and I were both very conscious of His presence. Her eyes followed us, as we waved goodbye.

That night, Molly passed into eternity, to meet the same Saviour who had said to the woman who had sinned, "Neither do I condemn thee, go and sin no more." No more the merciless stones of the world's condemnation, no more the pain of rejection, and the lash of scorn.

Molly would never have willingly taken her own life. She had sought relief in the tablets, and had become confused and irresponsible.

The only mourners were my wife and myself, and two of the lads from the homes. It was a wet, blustery April morning, and the cemetery was almost deserted as we waited in the rain. A solitary hearse drove up to the chapel, and a black-robed priest appeared from some secluded corner. He had an air of distaste for his job, and quickly recited his lines. We followed to the outskirts of the cemetery, to a public grave. There were no ornate headstones here. A couple of gravediggers were waiting at a discreet distance. Even the sparrows were

too absorbed with their preparations for spring to break
the silence with their twittering. The priest recited the
committal competently and meticulously, and hurried
away. The four of us gathered round the open grave. Our
voices, not rich in quality, but with emotion and full
hearts, joined in the sweet words:

> Safe in the arms of Jesus,
> Safe on His gentle breast,
> There by His love o'er shaded,
> Sweetly my soul shall rest.

We sang every verse of the hymn, and laid a solitary
wreath of spring flowers by the grave.

It is well to tell of our failures, and remember them.
Molly had been before the Courts. She was an ex-offender.
Hers was a sad story, and to some extent we share the
blame. We might have done just that little bit more. We
might have tried just that little bit harder to find someone
with sympathy, with a Christ-like love in their hearts, to
comfort this poor lonely soul. This is not an isolated case.
There are so many who have sunk to despair just because
nobody cared, or tried to understand. To those of us who
have mixed with the sub-strata of society, the alcoholics,
the drug-addicts, the persistent offenders, there is an overwhelming consciousness of the need for personal contact
and companionship, rather than counselling and direc-
tion. The sociologist, the psychiatrist and the psychologist
have studied their problems and case-histories, and have
written reports and treatises and erudite essays. There
have been conferences and committees, and classifica-
tions, suggestions and experiments, and still we have the

same pitiful parade of human misery in the Courts, or queuing outside the Crypt.

Let us remember Molly. Let us remember that she died because she had no kindly soul to whom she could turn in her hour of need, nobody to whom she could pour out her distress. Our Lord came to seek and to save that which was lost. May God grant that our "sanctification" be not submerged in sanctimonious respectability.

CHAPTER EIGHT

THE MALE NURSE WHO TURNED TO DRUGS

It is inevitable that at times we feel some degree of impatience and intolerance with the drug-addict and the alcoholic. So often, however, when we delve into the case-history, we realise the subtlety of the initial approach, and the innocence of the first involvement. I cannot but wonder whether we ourselves would have fared better, had we been enmeshed in similar circumstances.

Jim had never known his father. "I did not see very much of my mother either," he told me. "In her efforts to look after us she always seemed to be away at work. Nevertheless she was part of my daily life. I suppose she was more or less my anchor, and when the blow came I was entirely unprepared."

I was listening quietly at his bedside. He was recovering from a severe bout of delirium. A growth of black beard and his pallid face made him look older than his thirty years.

"It happened one day about ten years ago," he went on. "I had come home as usual from the training college, where I was studying nursing. I went into the living-room, and found a letter for me on the table. I can't tell you its contents, but it contained for me a great personal blow which left me a little dazed. Suddenly I heard a crash in the hall outside, and I went to see what had happened. I found my mother lying in the hall in a pool of blood. She was only semi-conscious. I think I lost my self-control. I threw my arms around her and cried to her to come back to me. She seemed to hear me and regained consciousness for a short time. Then she collapsed and died. I've only a hazy memory of what happened afterwards. I remember fetching a cushion and a glass of water, and getting a neighbour. Then everything went blank."

"The police told me there would have to be a post-mortem. Something in me resented the mutilation of the only person I had ever loved, and I bitterly opposed it, but they said that if I didn't consent they would get a Court Order. Going over her things I found tragic evidence of what she must have suffered, silently and uncomplainingly. Medical evidence discovered that she had secondary cancer of the liver, bladder and kidneys. I remember contacting a few members of the family, and there was a quiet funeral. The shock left me in complete confusion, and for days I wandered about aimlessly. Everything seemed meaningless and empty."

Jim was a native of Glasgow. He told me that after his mother's death, he decided to devote himself to his nursing career, and he was sent to a hospital in Scotland for training. It was there that he first developed a tremor in his right hand.

"I was finding increasing difficulty in writing my reports," he explained. "At first it was just an annoyance, and having a little medical knowledge, I decided to treat myself with barbiturates, and I took a small dose of sodium amytal. I found that the tremors disappeared, and I continued with small doses. Before long I was experiencing slight withdrawal symptoms, and the tremors became worse as the effect of the drug wore off. I started to increase the dose, and I soon realised that I should have to watch the accumulation of barbiturates in my system. I knew that there must be rest periods from the drug, and I arranged these at weekends, and off-duty times. This went on for six or seven weeks. Then, one day I went into the staff sitting-room and went to sit on a chair which was not there. I knew that this displacement of objects was one of the symptoms of barbiturate poisoning. My legs also would give way without warning, and I would fall. I always picked myself up quickly, and I thought that no one had noticed. My writing, however, had been affected, and I was doing a tremendous amount of overtime without any apparent fatigue. All this, I found out later, had been observed.

"One day I felt really ill, and as I struggled to get to my room I passed out completely. They fetched the principal, who was of course a doctor. He stated that they had been concerned about me for some time and I made a clean breast of things and told him what I had done. He was sympathetic and explained that the tremors were a result of delayed shock at my mother's death, and that if I had consulted a doctor he would have ordered complete rest, which would soon have cleared up the condition. For the sake of my nursing career the doctor said he would not put what I had done on record, and he arranged for me to have treatment. I spent some time in hospital, and came out (as I thought) cured. I went on well after this for nearly a year, and then found that I was having slight recurrences of the tremors. I tried small doses of sodium pentobarb, a much milder drug, but it wasn't so effective, and I found myself falling back on the sodium amytal. I knew the folly of it, but my problem was increasing, and the relief was at my elbow. I soon realised that I had become heavily addicted, but my training enabled me to control it up to a point, and I tried to be careful. I managed to complete three years training.

"It was then I had my next breakdown. I was on night duty in the nurses' home, and one of my colleagues indicated that he knew I was taking drugs. I was annoyed, and completely lost my temper. The excitement was too much for me and the next thing I knew I was on the floor and couldn't move. They fetched the doctor, and I had to confess that I was again in the same trouble. Once more arrangements were made for me to be admitted to hospital. I was put on a milder substitute drug, sodium pentothal, which resulted in my being in a sort of twilight sleep, where although I was aware of my surroundings, I was incapable of movement. The doctors asked me all sorts of questions during this period, and when I was finally discharged they told me that there had been no brain damage, for which I was grateful. I was able to return to my work, and I did a year's nursing at a general hospital in Glasgow. It was during this period that I first started on alcohol, and once more I was having recourse to drugs. I found now that I needed one or the other to get relief from my persistent tremors, which so handicapped my writing and interfered with my work. I thought that possibly a change of surroundings might help, and I applied for a post in mental health nursing. I was accepted, and moved to England, to take care of severely handicapped children.

This was in Berkshire. Unfortunately my tremors still persisted, and I was relying heavily on brandy, and still taking drugs. I loved my work, but I was very conscious of the emptiness of my life, and I had little or no incentive to fight my enemy."

As Jim continued, I saw him wipe away the beads of perspiration from his forehead, and I could not but notice the trembling of his hands.

"It was at this time," he went on, "that I had serious thoughts of suicide. I decided to move to mentally handicapped nursing, and was moved to a hospital in Hertfordshire. Time went on without any improvement, and my addiction to both alcohol and drugs escalated. The tremors were getting completely out of hand, and I was mentally tired. I did nearly succeed in taking my life, but this time it was not intentional. I was aware of the permissible intake of drugs, and I knew that I was reaching danger level, but there were periods of mental confusion, and during one of these I actually took an overdose. As I felt myself slipping away I realised what had happened. I staggered to my bed, incapable of anything and I thought it must be the end. I knew my only chance would be if I was found by one of the cleaners, a very poor chance. I lost consciousness. God's hand must have been over me then. A cleaner did come. She fetched the house doctor.

"I was unconscious for four days. They told me that in the ambulance my heart had stopped beating, that I was given oxygen, and that I was very lucky to be alive. I wished that they had not succeeded in bringing me back to life. I felt I just couldn't face going through the whole cycle again, and I'd rather it had ended that way, as an accident.

"I found myself in the Peace Memorial Hospital in Hertfordshire, and after some time they decided to send me to the Nerve Hospital in London. There they put me through exhausting tests, each of which was like having an operation without anaesthetic. Each one was an ordeal, and I felt I couldn't face much more. I was very low. At last the surgeon came to me. 'Well, Mr Downie,' he said, 'there is nothing that requires an operation, but damage has been done which only time can heal.' I would have preferred to have slipped quietly into oblivion.

"I went back to the hospital in Hertfordshire, to my nursing appointment, but the chief male nurse suggested that I should have a rest, remaining resident in the hospital. Unfortunately, I had quite a large quantity of drugs in my locker, and in my present frame of mind I was an easy prey to temptation. I took them. You just don't act reasonably once you become addicted and I didn't care much what happened.

"Eventually, I got an appointment at a geriatric hospital, and was soon put in charge of the ward. This proved my final undoing, as I now had charge of the drug cupboard. I did not know at the time that all drugs were checked. There came the day when the chief male nurse told me that matron wished to see me in her office. Quietly, she told me that certain drugs were missing and could not be accounted for. 'There are only two of you in charge of the keys,' she said, 'and I know that the other man is not responsible. What can you tell me of the matter? I leave it to you.' I knew, of course, that excuses were of no avail, and I told her the whole truth.

" 'I cannot tolerate this,' she said abruptly, 'you will have to go.' I knew this was the end. I went to get my bags, and took some more drugs. I had no idea what to do or where to go, but I remember that on my way out I passed a minister of some kind. I just remember he had a clerical collar. I must have looked pretty bad, because he stopped and said 'Is anything wrong?' I brushed past him and burst out crying. The next thing I knew I was sitting in the street with my trousers rolled up, slashing my legs with a razor blade. I was only semi-conscious, and wanted someone to take over. They must have taken me to a hospital. I remember being rather roughly handled, stripped and thrown into a padded cell. Only then did I plumb the depths of mental torture. I cried and struggled, even though I knew it was of no avail, and after what seemed to be endless hours, a nurse came and gave me an injection of paraldehyde, but I was already saturated with drugs, my body had had too much. I begged them not to lock me up, but the door closed on me again. By morning I was completely exhausted with my futile struggles, and when they again opened the door, I begged them to give me no more injections. I could not stand up, and I was carried to a bed in the ward.

"I was taken to Napsbury Hospital in Hertfordshire, and put in a ward with many other addicts. After some days, I was interviewed by a quiet-spoken man, who asked me what I considered to be rather stupid questions. I felt he was grossly under-rating my intelligence. After he had gone I asked the other patients who he was. They seemed a bit vague, but replied 'Every time he comes, somebody gets certified'. The idea that it might mean me did not dawn on me at first, but later the full impact of it came home. It was not long since I had been turning the key on others. Now it was to be turned on me. A wave of bitter resentment came over me, and I really went berserk, and smashed six windows, badly cutting my wrist. Two hefty male nurses came and overpowered me, and I was put in a straightjacket, tied in bed, and the bed clothes pulled up to my chin, so that no one could see I was trussed. I had six stitches in my wrist, and all I could do was to think things over. I realised the folly of trying to fight them, and when they gave me a tranquilliser I soon fell asleep. When I woke again, I assured them I had no intention of causing any further trouble. They released me and I was put back in my own bed.

"I managed to see the Welfare Officer, and I told him what had happened. He promised to look into things. Soon I had an apology from the medical staff. They explained that they had not had my full medical history available. I was assured that I would not be locked up again, and I was transferred to an open ward. By now I could no longer use my right hand, and I had to be fed. I tried to train myself, but I had virtually no control, and couldn't even use a spoon. I was once more, however, treated as an intelligent person.

"After some weeks, power came back to my hand and I was gradually able to feed myself, and even make my own bed. I was given occupational therapy to get back the use of my fingers, and I started making toy animals. The doctors seemed satisfied with my progress, and I was recommended for rehabilitation, but I was told very firmly that my nursing career was finished.

"I went to the rehabilitation centre, and after a short stay, I was able to get a job with a firm of painters in Coventry, after getting temporary accommodation in a flat. I started to drink heavily again, first at night after work, then in the mornings as well, carrying a bottle of brandy to work with me, and taking things to disguise my breath. I managed to get some drugs, and this cut my drinking down a little, but soon I was heavily involved with both. I just managed to pay for my flat, but everything else was going in drink, drugs and cigarettes. I also began to sell my few possessions. I was taking little or no food, and one night I found that I could no longer have my flat. I walked the streets that night, after spending practically all I had on drink and drugs, and at 2 a.m. I collapsed from the combined effects of alcohol, drugs and fatigue. Someone found me, and wanted to take me to hospital, but I refused. I managed to get to the place where I worked, and spent the rest of the night in the builder's yard. I asked the foreman next day if he could get me a place, and with the help of one of the workmen, I managed to get another flat. My work was deteriorating, but I just couldn't break with the bottle. Finally, I had to give up my job. I was too ill to work, and I had to go to a doctor. He immediately arranged for me to be admitted to Coventry General Hospital. They diagnosed barbiturate poisoning, aggravated by excessive drinking. I was put on the usual withdrawal treatment, a substitute drug (always an ordeal), and given vitamins to restore my strength. The doctor told me they had no facilities for the type of treatment I needed, and after a while, I was discharged and placed in the care of the Mental Health Department. I managed to get a job of sorts, but I was only concerned with getting drugs and brandy. I was losing the ability to earn money, and soon left the job. I was in pretty desperate straits, and went to the local branch of Alcoholics Anonymous. I was told the usual things, "It's up to you, we haven't any magic pills". I applied for a post in the GPO, and sat an exam, which I passed, and I thought this might be a chance. However, they insisted on a medical examination, and I was sent to a neurologist in Birmingham. His report must have been pretty bad, because I was immediately turned down. Dejectedly, I went back to the Labour Exchange, and found that I had been put on the disabled persons' register. They sent me after several jobs, but always the same story, 'Sorry, you're just too late, but if there is anything else, we'll get in touch with you'.

"I went to stay with some people in Coventry who had for a time befriended me, and I applied to the National Assistance Board for help. I just had to get money in some way for drink and drugs. It was all I had left. I went again to the Labour Exchange, and they seemed shocked at my condition, and told me I was too ill to work.

" 'Get home', they said, 'and we will arrange for the District Nurse to visit you.'

"I still had the keys of the flat, and I went back there with despair in my heart, sick in body and soul. They must have advised the Mental Health Officer, because he came and found me there. He said I must go back into hospital. I thought I couldn't last much longer, and didn't much care, except that I had a dread of being cut off from drugs and alcohol. I remember being in an ambulance, and arriving at All Saints Hospital in Birmingham. I remember crying out for a drink . . . and then my first bout of delirium tremens. I saw huge spiders, insects blown up to fantastic sizes, crawling everywhere. Monstrosities in awful detail. Only those who have known the real horror of it can realise what I went through."

It was at this stage that I first met Jim. He was only semi-conscious, and his moans and cries were piteous, and were having an adverse effect on the other patients. As soon as he regained full consciousness, I was asked by the staff to talk to him. We soon became good friends, the beginning of a long association. I told him of the only One who could really meet his need. He listened attentively, and we had many talks.

He made good progress, and I was disappointed later to learn that he had discharged himself. He had seemed willing to make the effort to pull himself together, and I had hoped that we could have found him accommodation with us in Birmingham, and given him the support he so urgently needed. Jim went back to his flat, and in spite of all his resolutions he returned to drugs and drink. Again things went from bad to worse, and on a Sunday evening he decided once again to end it all in oblivion. He told me afterwards that he remembered swallowing a large quantity of barbiturates, reaching the borderline of the fatal dose. His memory of what happened afterwards was very hazy, but he suddenly decided to make for my place in Birmingham, and somehow managed to get to Coventry Station.

"I saw that the restaurant bar was open," he told me, "and I remember having an overpowering urge to get brandy. I knew this would be the end for me, after all the barbiturates. If ever I was on the brink of the pit, I was then. I remember making a feeble cry to God for help. I rushed out of the station. A taxi-driver was waiting outside, and I asked him how much he would charge to take me to Birmingham. He said £2.50. I told him I had £2.00. That taxi-driver must have had a heart of gold. He saw my desperate state and agreed to take me, but I couldn't remember your address. I gave him a card with your telephone number."

The taxi-driver phoned me at about 9.30 p.m. on the Sunday evening. I directed him how to reach our home, and in about twenty minutes he was at my door. He was indeed a kind and sympathetic chap, and between us we managed to get Jim to a room.

He was in a bad way, and I knew he needed medical attention. I phoned the charge nurse at All Saints, and it was agreed he should be admitted. We managed to get him into my car, and by 11 p.m. he was back again in the hospital.

To the normal person the torment he had endured, and the punishment he had taken, would have been sufficient to drive home the lesson. We talked about his future, and he readily agreed that from then on a rigid and total abstinence from drugs and alcohol was the only solution to his problem. A new and well-ordered pattern, a really firm resolve for the years ahead.

Within three weeks Jim had again discharged himself, and was back in Coventry . . . back on drugs . . . back on drink . . . I had no idea where he had gone, and we lost touch.

Once again he was brought back in a deplorable condition to the drug-addiction unit at All Saints Hospital. He was in a dazed state, and it seemed that the sight of the charge nurse brought back to him the reality of his situation, and the horrors of his last experience. Somehow he managed to get a razor, and slashed his wrists.

"I remember a struggle," Jim told me afterwards, "and then the next thing I remember is that I was in a private locked ward on the mental side."

The staff in the Unit told me what had happened, and I finally managed to locate him. There was a look of mute despair in his eyes, but he seemed relieved to see me. He implored me to help him. He had an overwhelming horror of being "certified". I was able to reassure Jim on this point, and after a short period he was again transferred to the addiction unit, with its freedom of action. On the following Sunday, I persuaded him to accompany us to the evening service at the Zion Mission in Handsworth. The minister, Pastor McCulloch, a saintly man, made a moving and powerful appeal, and at the end of the service he asked that anyone who was really seeking a commitment to Christ should raise their hand. To my surprise and relief, Jim raised his. Previously he had always refused to make any definite decision, although he had always listened and agreed when I spoke to him of God. I knew this time he meant it. That night he committed his life to Christ.

"For the first time in my life", he told me afterwards, "I knew peace. Christ had entered my life, and I knew release from the abject slavery of my previous existence."

Jim spent a short time at Hill Farm. The tremors which had distressed him for so long soon ceased, and he was able to resume work. His life has seen many vicissitudes since that day, but he has held on to his faith, and is no longer haunted and harrowed by the cravings and torments of his early life. He has consented to telling his story, that we may have a glimpse into the twilight life of the addict, and that we may be moved with compassion for their sorry state. Thousands have brought themselves to this state by their own stupidity, or by selfish self-indulgence. Thousands have become unwittingly enmeshed, sometimes through circumstances over which they had no control. One heart-cry is common to all, "set me free".

CHAPTER NINE

FACE-TO-FACE WITH CHRIST IN PRISON

There is an illusion among so many Christian people, that having persuaded a man or woman to accompany them to their church or chapel, and having seen them break down under the power of the gospel message, and surrender their lives to Christ, the great miracle has happened, and their long and maybe arduous work is ended. The great miracle has indeed happened, the miracle of new birth, but they are so often apt to forget that the new converts are indeed "babes in Christ", and in vital need of nurturing, protecting, and feeding. They need patience and understanding and love when they stumble and fall, even as a child taking its first faltering steps needs to be lifted up, helped and encouraged.

Colin told me his story soon after he joined our staff at Adullam. It was of his early feeble efforts to walk a new road, and of a ready hand outstretched to help when he fell. He began with his childhood days.

"As a boy" he said, "my first recollections of religion were of being sent with my two brothers to Mass at St. Francis" Church in Manchester. Mum and Dad used to give us our collection money, and pack us off, but the nearest we

got to the church was the 'old blind man's shop' across the
road from St. Francis. While one of us went to see what
colour of garment the priest was wearing, the other two
would spend the collection money on 'goodies' from the
shop. When we got home, we knew we should be asked
what colour garments the priest was wearing, and we were
ready with the answer. Being good Catholics, our parents
were making sure that our souls were cared for, but we seldom went as a family, and I'm afraid I lost interest very
quickly, even to the point of not bowing, and making the
sign of the Cross when I went past the church.

"The next time I had anything to do with religion", he
continued, "was when I was nearing the end of a two-year
prison sentence."

There was an almost unacceptable incongruity in his
words. It seemed incomprehensible that the tall clear-eyed
fresh-complexioned young man in front of me, with his
obvious concern for our work, and the sincerity of his
Christian faith, should have been himself involved with the
law. It was with manifest distaste that he spoke of his past.

"Lots of things happened between those years," he went
on. "Drugs, hospitals, borstals, and now this. I started taking drugs when I went with my friends to an 'all-night'
club every Saturday night. The only way to stay up all
night was to take amphetamines. We liked them, or rather
we liked the effects of them, and soon we wanted them
not only on Saturday night, but every night. We wanted to
be up all the time if possible. Of course it led to me breaking into a chemist's shop, and finding myself on the wrong
side of the law."

He hesitated. I appreciated his reticence, but I pressed
him to continue.

"You see," Colin said, "when you are on a certain drug, it is unusual if you don't come in contact with people taking other drugs. That's how it was with me. I was introduced to cannabis, barbiturates, and 'acid'. After taking quite a few 'trips', I didn't seem to relate any more to my parents, or to my 'straight' friends. The only place where I could find understanding and companionship was within the drug 'scene'.

"I remember going home after one 'trip' and just sitting upstairs crying because nobody seemed able to understand me. I knew my parents loved and cared, but I just couldn't get through to them what the drugs were doing to me, and how I felt about life. It was shortly after this that I started to use the 'needle', and everything that goes with it. All my days were spent trying to get away from myself with the aid of anything that I could inject. In between times I had served a couple of sentences in borstal. There had been no effort at rehabilitation, and now I was sitting in prison, with only one thought, to head straight for my drug 'friends' on release, and to get more dope.

"This was all before Jesus took a hold on my life. In prison, I used to knock around with all the guys from Manchester that I knew. One day it was announced that Cliff Richard and some Christian people from Birmingham would be coming to the prison. We knew the sort of stuff they would be giving us, and at first we thought 'Well, they won't see us there', but as the time for their visit came nearer we thought it might be an excellent opportunity to have some fun, taking the 'mickey' out of them, and maybe seeing some girls. Well that's all we did do at the first meeting, but suddenly one of the guys got converted, and I got curious. I used to wait till nobody was around and then ask him about it. He seemed to have found something that was real, but I thought it couldn't be for me. Somehow, I was being made aware of a conscience, and for me this was really something. Gradually, however, I again lost interest, and I didn't bother to attend any more meetings.

"One night I was standing at the back of the television room, watching *Top of the Pops*, when one of the Christian people came in and asked me why I hadn't been back to the meetings. I made up an excuse, but he wasn't to be put off. He asked me to come with him to the meeting that night. My head was swimming with all sorts of reasons why I should not go, but somehow I found myself walking along beside him. When we got to the room a singing group was on, and one of the songs was 'Why don't you learn to tell the truth?' That song really hit me. I never told the truth, and my whole life was a lie, and a shambles. I can't remember what actually happened, but that night I asked Jesus to come into my life. He did. In spite of what happened afterwards, he came to me that night. For the next two weeks the prison officers, whom I used to hate, were amazed at the change they saw in me. They knew something had happened, but what it was, they were not quite sure.

"The real test came on my release. I went home armed with Bibles, books, and a new faith. It was a critical period and just at that time I had no one to turn to. I was very vulnerable and very weak. The temptations were just around the corner, and I soon fell, and was back taking drugs. I had known a girl for a long time, and we decided to get married. Both of us started using 'hard drugs' again. The problem was that I was running away, not only from myself, but from Jesus, but 'the soul that on Jesus has leaned for repose, he'll never, no never, desert to its foes'. After many feeble attempts on our own to stop the drugs, my wife and I decided to ask for help. We were told of the Life for the World organisation, a Christian community which helped addicts and we applied to them, and were accepted. We spent a few months in their company, and then decided to leave, not feeling one bit better than when we arrived. We were both thoroughly disheartened, and feeling desperate. There seemed little else that we could now do. We both realised the futility of our lives, but could not rid ourselves of the craving. Something possessed us which could not be exorcised. After many struggles, we decided that our only chance was to ask the Life for the World people to take us back. They agreed, but only on the condition that we were separated. Debbie, my wife, would have to go to a girls' place, and I would have to stay at the main centre. The first couple of months were terrible, with both Debbie and myself threatening to leave every weekend. We really missed each other, but there was now a hunger in our hearts for a new life, and Jesus gave us the strength to fight on. It was at the Life for the World centre that we both finally surrendered, and opened our hearts to the Lord, and let him take over our lives."

Colin did not tell us much about the final battle with himself, but he was deeply appreciative of the help he had received at this critical period of his life. He paid a warm tribute to the young Christian man who had taken him, almost against his will, to the meeting in prison where he had made his first decision.

"He continually helped me after my release from prison," Colin told me, "and through all the bad times we went through. He would think nothing of driving to Manchester in the middle of the night, just to say that someone cared, and that God still loved us. Yes, for that I'm really grateful, because when a Christian gets involved with a drug-addict, it's not just a matter of conversion and hallelujah. It needs an awful lot of love, patience and perseverance to see that person make it."

As Colin told me his story, I was very grateful that he had joined us. At last we had someone who knew the tensions and the stresses, and the tortured mind of the addict, and who had first-hand knowledge of the deep-seated emotional upheaval consistent with the physical withdrawal. Colin has the right approach to our problem. He is forthright, but with an understanding and compassion born of his own personal experience, and there is a deep thankfulness in his heart for the all-embracing love which brought him through.

"God has been with us both through all the dark days," he told us, "through all those days when we wanted to 'pack it in'. He never changed, and he was always there to lift us up, with his everlasting love."

Colin now has a home and a young family, and is a member of his local Baptist church. He is doing the type of work which he wanted to do, and for which he seems so well-fitted, dedicating his life to the service of the Lord. Yes, he knows and understands the people with whom we deal at Adullam. He has found the answer to the problem of his life, his "raison d'être".

How different it might have been, but for the intervention and persistence of the young man who refused to be deterred by apparent failure. We are slow to learn our lessons, and lives are often at stake. An impatient gesture or a hasty word at a critical point, may shatter and destroy our most earnest endeavours. It is too easy to shrug off our opportunities when it is at the cost of our own comfort and convenience.

CHAPTER TEN

THE STORY OF A BROKEN PEN

The first formative years of a child's life so often shape his future. Little Ben was a surly youngster, and not very popular at school. He was rather backward in the classroom, and unresponsive to the efforts of his teachers. He appeared to be resentful of the approaches of his fellow pupils. They didn't know just how much he wanted to be liked and loved. They did not know that he had a father who was so often the worse for drink, often violent, a father whom he feared, and from whom he so often fled. They did not know that his mother had to bear the whole burden of a large family, and be the main provider. She worked from morning till night to earn sufficient food for a family of eight, and therefore had little time for the goodnight kiss, and the tender caress. She had an indomitable courage, but so little time for love. Ben was often hungry, sometimes for food, but more often hungry for someone who really loved and cared for him. He felt that he didn't matter very much to anyone, and he knew that his instinctive urge to show affection would be met with rebuffs, and from his father maybe curses and a blow.

If his teachers and fellow pupils had known the yearning in Ben's heart, it might never have happened. It was near the end of term, and the morning class was almost over. The teacher held up a brand new fountain-pen, taken out of coloured tissue paper, in a brightly coloured box.

"I'm going to give this pen to some boy in this class," she said. "but this time I want every boy to have an equal chance of winning. I know that we can't all win prizes, and so often the same boys seem to win them, but this time it won't matter whether you have done your homework or not."

It was an "end-of-term" gesture, prompted no doubt by the holiday spirit of goodwill. The teacher meant well. Ben noticed a few black hairs that protruded from the side of her mouth. She was a model of prim austerity.

"I'm going to give each boy a number," she went on, "I've got two of every number, one lot in one hat and one lot in another. All the numbers will be shaken up. Then I'm going to pass one of the hats round, and each boy will take one number. When you've all got a number, I'm going to let someone pick a number out of the other hat, and he'll call it out. Whoever has that number will get the pen." There was a subdued murmur of excitement.

With a smile of condescension she took the hat round to each row, and every boy eagerly took a little folded paper. Ben took out the small white missive, and furtively unfolded it. He saw the number. It was fourteen. He looked around the large classroom, and wondered who would win. He had never owned a pen, but the nuns had told him that God always over-ruled these things, and of course God knew all about him, that he was the lowest in the class, and he had never been very good. No, it wouldn't be him.

The teacher, in her starched white linen, was speaking again. She called one of the boys by name, and he stepped out to the front. She picked up the other hat.

"Now pick out one number only," she said with her customary note of authority. The boy picked one out.

"What is the number?" she asked.

"Fourteen."

"Now stand up the boy with number fourteen."

Ben's grip tightened on the little crumpled piece of paper. He stood up. Everybody was looking at him. Envy? Admiration? He didn't care. No great potentate ever had a prouder moment. The world was watching him. It was watching Ben Smith, it was no longer revolving on its axis. He was transfixed in a few moments of ecstasy.

He didn't realise that the teacher was talking to him, until she approached his desk. Then he saw the scorn in her eyes.

". . . and of all the boys in this class, you're the most undeserving, and we're all sorry that it's you . . ."

She pushed the pen unceremoniously in front of him. He wanted to cry, but a fierce resentment held back the tears. Napoleon had faced his Waterloo with fortitude, but then he'd had years of glory, and Ben had only had a few brief moments. He was shattered and humiliated. And he was only ten years old. He put the pen in his pocket, and sat down, gripping it, crushing it. The class was dismissed, and Ben wandered out into the street alone. He hurled the pen in the path of the oncoming traffic. It was smashed to fragments.

It was some thirty years later when we first met. Ben was serving a sentence in Winson Green Prison. On my first visit he was in the punishment cell, but through the good offices of a kindly welfare officer, I was able to talk to him. From the first, there seemed to be a mutual attraction, and we were soon firm friends. He told me the story of the pen. The wound had never healed, and he was now a confirmed alcoholic, and had a background of thirty-two convictions for offences committed either under the influence of drink, or to obtain it. There was a latent urge within him to destroy the things he most loved. Drink liberated and inflamed this urge, causing him to be rejected by his family, and ostracised by society. As he told me of his past, I could not but recognise an underlying sincerity and honesty in all he said. They were not the shifty, averted eyes of the average thief that met mine. He looked me straight in the eye, and we were soon exchanging confidences. It was a sad tale he told. His father had died a drunkard's death, and his only remaining friend, his mother, had also died. The rest of the family had already left home. Piece by piece, the furniture had been sold for drink.

He told me of public-house brawls, of how he smashed the windows of the offices of the Social Security, because they would not give him the cash which he considered was his due. He told me of his borrowing from his brothers, sums of money which were never paid back. Of pawning his brother's suit, and his brother's kindness and tolerance. He never concealed the more sordid elements of his story – always the overpowering urge for liquor dominating his life, all defeating, overwhelming, and always cropping up and regurgitating, the incident of the pen. He had built up a barrier of defiance against the world. There was no hint of self-pity. Like Ishmael, his hand was against every man, and every man's hand against him. At least, that seemed to be his philosophy when I first knew him. There was always an innate strength of character, and a courage which I could not but admire. He told me of the time his courage failed him.

It was Christmas Eve, and Ben was in the house alone. All that was left was a dirty mattress, and a few old coats, and the TV set. He liked to watch television in his sober moments, but he knew he must have a drink, and he had only a few coppers left. He went to one of the few pubs where he still could be served. He had been turned out of most of them in the area. He approached an acquaintance.

"Want to buy a TV set, Joe?" Joe eyed him with some suspicion.

"Yours?"

"Yes." Ben showed no resentment at the implied aspersion of his integrity.

"How much?"

"Two quid."

"I'll see it."

Within fifteen minutes, Ben had arrived back with the TV set in his arms. The bargain was struck, and the cash paid over. By closing time, Ben had spent every penny, and was hopelessly, stupidly drunk.

Christmas morning found Ben on his mattress, his head aching, cold and penniless. The gas had been turned off. There was no food in the house, no tea, and no milk. Nothing but the bare walls, for the wallpaper was peeling off with the damp. He buried his head in the mattress, and wept. That day, he plumbed greater depths of despair than he had ever known. He spent a few hours wandering round empty streets, then the long dark hours without sleep. He was too weak, and too weary, to attempt a "break-in", and anyway, there were too many people at home at Christmas.

The following morning, hungry and dejected, he found a coffee shop open. He begged for something to eat, and the woman at the counter, her heart moved with pity, cooked him a plateful of sausage and egg.

Several weeks in arrears of rent, Ben had to leave the only place he knew as home, and he began a life of dossing in derelict houses, with the occasional night in the Crypt, a free night shelter for the homeless.

Ben was always reticent about his crimes. There were many charges of assault, but they were usually after a quarrel in the pub, or an assault on the police. In most cases, it was Ben who carried the marks of combat, and who bore the brunt of the conflict. He would never attack a person weaker than himself. He had his own code of ethics. He did, however, manage to augment his meagre resources by occasional "break-ins", but it was so often followed by a period in the nick. He was too well known to authority. Many nights were spent in a derelict house in an area due for demolition. He preferred a room upstairs, and after a heavy drinking bout, he managed to find his way to his usual haunt. He was far too befuddled to realise that demolition work had started. He groped up the shaky, but familiar stairs, and stepped into his room. Something gave way beneath him, and he vaguely remembers crashing down to the floor below. He was unconscious for a time. Bruised and bloody, but with no broken bones, he recovered sufficiently to crawl out before workmen arrived. A passer-by saw his condition, and offered to phone for an ambulance, but Ben would have none of it. He went and washed his wounds under the tap in a public toilet. On another occasion, after a collapse in the street, he was taken to hospital. They found he had pneumonia, due to exposure. He recovered sufficiently to get out of bed, and promptly discharged himself, despite the threats and warnings of the nurse and doctor.

Ben came to us on his discharge from prison. He did not easily make friends, but he got along quite well with a young man just out of Detention Centre, and in spite of an occasional binge, he managed to live a normal life for some months. It was the beginning of a rather chequered period in his life spending much of his time with us, but alternating with bouts of dissipation. His clashes with the law, however, were becoming less and less frequent. When we finally had to leave Newhaven, it was Ben that urged me to start again. He was aggressively insistent, brusquely brushing aside all my objections. He was one of the first residents in our first home, a pioneer of Adullam, and we asked him to become a member of our first committee. This, unfortunately, did not prove an outstanding success. His criticism of the other members was in the vernacular, and couched in no uncertain terms. His suggestions on general policy were also rather drastic.

Ben was always suspicious of anything which savoured of preferential treatment for any of the men. Two of them had spent an evening at my home, and had stayed rather late. Maybe he thought he should have been included, and to prove his point he spent the evening in the pub, although he had been off the drink for some time. About 10.30 p.m. the telephone rang. It was Ben, his voice rather slurred.

"It's Ben." He sounded uncompromising and truculent. "Yer'd better come over," he said, "an' you'll find it all smashed up."

"What's the matter?" There was an ominous click. The conversation had ended abruptly. With the two young men I went over to investigate. The four panes in the window of the sitting-room had been broken, and the glass was strewn over the carpet. There was no sign of Ben. The men did a rapid clean-up, and drew the curtains over the window. The police arrived shortly afterwards. Ben had been to the police station to tell them that he had smashed up the house, and a police car had been sent to see the damage.

"What's the trouble?" they enquired briskly.

"What trouble?" asked one of the young men, with a look of bland innocence. He invited them in.

"We've had a report of some damage being done to this house."

The two officers looked around. Everything seemed normal, and reasonably tidy. The curtains were covering the broken windows. There was no apparent sign of anything untoward.

"He must have been pulling our leg," the officer remarked wryly. "Maybe he wanted to spend the night in the lock-up." They refused the offer of a cup of tea, and left, apparently satisfied. By 3 a.m. a rather subdued Ben arrived home, and went to bed. The next day he insisted on paying for the damage out of his own pocket.

Although Ben had a very hard exterior, he had a tender heart. His seemingly churlish manner was so often a camouflage for a sensitive and sentimental nature. With the elderly and infirm he was compassionate and self-sacrificing. He was rather gauche and unorthodox in expression, and appeared to be almost ashamed of some kindly little act. He loved children, but just could not relate to them. He also loved all animals, so we finally managed to get him a dog. They became devoted friends. The dog would accept his blackest moods without condemnation or criticism. Its welcome was just as loving and loyal whether Ben came home drunk or sober. Somehow the dog fulfilled a need, a need to be accepted in any circumstance, and under all conditions. His dog was never hungry. When the week's allowance had been thrown away on drink and cigarettes, there was always an ample supply of dog food on the shelves, and if, on rare occasions, the budget could be stretched to include a small joint of meat, the major portion would inevitably end up on the plate under the table, or be snatched from his willing fingers.

Ben staunchly protested that he was a Roman Catholic, but he would often join us in our nightly worship service. He loved the hymns, with a special preference for those relating to the Cross, and to our Lord's sacrifice. "There is a green hill far away" was undoubtedly his favourite. He always showed a deep reverence, and often intense emotion. He hated any form of hypocrisy, and would never make an open confession of his faith. Neither were his heart stirrings always related to the environment of our meetings. He would recall incidents in the pub, sometimes seemingly irrelevant, when some words of a sacred song or hymn would be mentioned, and remorse would bring the tears welling up in his eyes. Somehow, you could not but believe him when he related these stories. In his blackest moods he was exasperating, churlish and defiant, unreasonable in argument, and unrelenting in his hate. He seemed hell-bent on antagonising his best friends, and you despaired of ever reaching the depths of his inner soul, until a flash of impish humour, or some sentimental confiding, betrayed the chink in his armour, and exposed a soft and vulnerable interior. You loved him and loathed him with disconcerting frequency, and with his alternating moods.

Twice more he broke a window, and replaced it at his own expense. Twice more he left us, and came back. I'm grateful for the day we first met. We had so much to learn from each other in the hard school of life, and I look forward to our meeting in the Great Beyond, and maybe hear him tell again the story of the broken pen, this time with a heart of forgiveness, and in the knowledge that "all things work together for good to those . . . who are called according to his purpose" (Romans 8:28), and when the last shall be first, and the first last. When the "Bens" of this world will be more esteemed maybe than the bishops.

It will soon be five years since his last brush with the law, and he prefers to forget the past. He has a home of his own, and is living the life of an ordinary citizen. That is why I do not give his real name. He is always ready and willing to succour anyone or anything weaker than himself, but he still resents any form of officiousness, and there is still evidence of that spirit of defiance against authority. The years are mellowing him, and over his life is the shadow of the Cross, and the love of a crucified Saviour.

CHAPTER ELEVEN

SHIPS THAT PASS IN THE NIGHT

I like to maintain contact with our people after they leave us, but some drift away to other towns or areas, and they do not find communication easy. They are "ships that pass in the night", a few short weeks maybe, and they are gone. They all know what we stand for, and what we believe. We try to show that we are a caring people, that we have love and compassion even for the most unlovable and unlovely. How far we succeed is in the hands of a righteous Judge. We sometimes have apparent failures, but we try to sow seeds which could lie dormant for years, and yet some future time germinate and bear fruit. God knows when the water of life will touch the dry ground.

I first met Malcolm in Winson Green Prison. He was in "solitary confinement", for his own protection. He had committed the unforgivable sin of "grassing" (telling tales about another inmate), or so it was alleged. He was a very frightened, fair-haired, pale-faced youth of nineteen, nearly due for discharge. He had already served a term in borstal, and for a similar offence, taking and driving away cars, but this time it had been coupled with an offence of "breaking and entering". He told me that his parents had refused to have him back home. I listened to his story, full of the customary excuses, and then he told me of his child-hood. The more trivial details convinced me of its truth. He was a twin, and his father had wanted a daughter. There were already three lively sons in the family, and the arrival of two more was a severe disappointment.

"My Dad always hated me," Malcolm said. "He used to beat me for anything at all. I often used to get bashed for the things my brothers had done." Malcolm's mother had died when he was five, and his father had married again. His stepmother appeared to share his father's resentment. When he was eight years old he was knocked down by a car, suffering rather severe injuries, and was in hospital for several weeks.

"Nobody ever came to see me," he said. "One day an elderly man came to the ward, and saw me crying. He asked me what was wrong, and I told him that my Mum and Dad had left me. I thought that they had. He was very kind, and said he'd come again to see me. He did, and brought me a train set. I'd never had anything like that before. I couldn't play with it in the hospital, but I kept tak-ing out the pieces and looking at them, and longing for the time when I could get back home and play with it there. Then my Dad came, at last. He didn't stay long, but he saw the train set by my bed. "What's this?" he asked. I told him about the kind man who had brought it. "You ain't 'avin it," he told me, and without even saying goodbye, he put it under his arm, and walked out. I never saw it again, and after that I knew I really hated him. I never forgave him. I remember crying most of the night after he'd gone."

It would be foolish to ascribe Malcolm's record of juve-nile and adolescent delinquency to this one cruel act by his father, but it most certainly left a wound which had never healed. The story he told us only underlined and emphasised the urgent need of a child for parental love, and illustrates the tragic consequences of its absence. It was the same sordid story that we hear so often in the courts. Stealing a few sweets from the corner shop, and then coins from a till, or from an unsuspecting pocket. In their later teens there comes the urge to drive a car and they soon learn how to manipulate the door locks, and how to start the engine. Their sense of moral value is warped, and any conscience these young folk may have had has been effectively silenced. If they get away unpunished at the first or second attempt, it boosts their ego and their confidence, and makes repentance and rehabilitation more unlikely.

Malcolm was not yet hardened in crime when he came to us, and we felt we were getting along wonderfully well with great hopes for the future, until his twin brother was discharged from jail. They decided to live together, but, unfortunately, his brother was the dominant partner. Both left us, and we were unable to trace them.

David's story had many similarities. He had had a very unhappy childhood, and there had been continual quarrelling in the family circle, both between the parents, and amongst the more adult members of the family. His father, although not an alcoholic, was a heavy drinker, and had been often ill-tempered and morose. His two sisters were children of an earlier marriage and disliked David. Consequently he felt rather isolated. He was afraid of his father, and the mother appeared to have been a rather weak woman, prone to occasional outbursts of temper, and showing little affection for him. He acquired the smoking habit at an early age, and this made an ever increasing demand on his resources. He was dismissed from his first job on suspicion of theft. Before long he was before the Juvenile Court, and was placed on probation. Further offences followed, with the inevitable sequence of detention centre, borstal and prison. At nineteen, when we first met, he had quite a formidable record.

David was with us nearly three months. In many ways we, on the staff, tried to show him that we cared, and that we were always there to help in time of need. His rent was usually in arrears, but we did not exert any undue pressure. He suddenly disappeared, and at the same time the hired TV set was also missing. We were compelled to report the loss under the rental agreement. David was arrested shortly afterwards, and he confessed to the theft. On his appearance in court we engaged our own solicitor to enter plea of mitigation, supported by a letter from us pleading his cause, and assuring the court of our willingness to reinstate him in our Home if they saw fit to give him his liberty. He was placed on probation, and he was returned to us, apparently penitent. Before long he was again in arrears with his rent, and when we protested he became truculent, and shortly afterwards left us. An ungrateful young layabout? That would seem to be a fairly adequate description of this young man.

Some six months later I was alone in the office. I saw a car draw up outside, and shortly afterwards the door-bell rang. I answered it. A very smartly-dressed young man stood outside, and he handed me a neat parcel.

"Sorry I can't stop," he said, "I'm late for an appointment."

He hurried back to his car and was gone, almost before I had recognised him. It was David.

The parcel was addressed to me. It was a brand new copy of *The New English Bible* carefully wrapped in cellophane. I opened the flyleaf, and inside was written my name, and "Thanks for all you did, and I'm sorry I let you down".

I never saw David again. I would like him to know that I'd like to say "Sorry" too. Sorry that my assessment of him was so hasty, sorry that I did not remember the sad, searing years of his childhood, starved of love, and very lonely. We learn our lessons in the Cave of Adullam.

It is sometimes hard to pinpoint the basic cause of a drift into crime. The Prison Welfare asked us to see George, and described him as "a forelock-touching little man". He was a thin-faced little chap, slightly balding, about forty-five years of age. He had a shocking record of convictions, mainly for theft. George came from a very respectable working-class home, but his parents were both dead, and his appalling record had estranged him from the other members of the family. We do not like to appear to probe into a man's antecedents, and he seemed unwilling to talk about his childhood, or indeed about any of his past. He had no home, and nowhere to go on his discharge, so we managed to find him accommodation.

George very quickly settled down. He was an outstanding craftsman, and his ability to manipulate locks was phenomenal. We tried to employ his talents, and divert them into more socially acceptable channels. He seemed quite anxious to co-operate, and we were able to offer him temporary employment. He was an odd character. He did not drink or smoke, and as far as we were aware, had no friends, either male or female. He appeared to have no hobbies, and showed no interest in any sport, or in any form of gambling.

We never seemed able to penetrate beyond the façade of polite acquiescence. He agreed with anything we said, but was always entirely self-sufficient. He showed no sign of a change of heart, and finally obtained a bachelor flat. George, however, has never been again in trouble. It is three years since his last conviction.

More distressing, but in many ways similar, was the case of John. He was a tall, cadaverous looking chap, well over fifty. He was recommended to us by a prison officer. He was in every way a model resident, and could do decorating, carpentry or bricklaying with equal facility. He liked a drink, but could always carry his liquor. He seemed to have a natural dignity, and we could never quite understand his lapse into crime, but he had spent many years in jail. He was with us for several months, and we hoped he had turned the corner, and found a better way of life. We always tried to recompense him for any work he did, but he always accepted any payment with an air of tolerance and condescension, as if bestowing a favour, much as royalty might graciously accept a gift from some humble subject.

One day we found his room empty. We contacted his probation officer, but there was no trace of him. The following day we found that his house had been opened during the night, and some things were missing, including the TV set. We never traced them, but shortly afterwards we were told John was again "inside". That was the last we heard of him. We felt we had failed. It is hard to find the remedy for the recidivist, and rehabilitation is a long hard slog, but we continue to work and pray.

We did with Ned, and so often we seemed on the very threshold of success, only to meet again with frustration and disappointment. We first met Ned in 1968, a tall, dark and austere looking man, who had spent many years at sea. He was an inveterate alcoholic, and his bouts of drinking invariably led to burglary and theft. When sober, he was quite a likeable chap, and would talk intelligently and seriously on most topics. He had served prison sentences in many parts of the world, and was well aware of his weakness. He told us he had tried many cures, including brain surgery, but to no avail. He stayed with us intermittently for short periods over the ensuing years, alternating with short or longer stays in prison. We maintained contact, wrote to him and visited him when "inside". His letters were always full of remorse and apparent repentance and each time on the completion of a sentence, there was the same resolution and the same determination to start afresh. I never doubted his sincerity, but I knew he was so very vulnerable. On one occasion, we went to London to meet him at the prison gates, and escort him to our home. The next day he was back in the pub, and had soon spent every penny he had received on his discharge. There were sometimes weeks of total abstinence when our hopes would be raised, but sooner or later there would be another lapse, and another house or shop would be broken into, and the well-known finger-prints left in profusion over the most obvious places. His blatant clumsiness proved that his crimes were never premeditated. He was an abject slave to his addiction.

Ned would spend the long hours of his confinement in the cell in forming grandiose plans for his future.

"This is the last time I shall see the inside of these walls," he would assure me. After a little training in some craft, usually some branch of the building trade, he would be quite confident that he had become an efficient trades-man.

"Give me some old house," he would insist, "and in a month's time you won't know it. It'll be the best house you've got."

Three times we took him at his word, and in a month's time the place was usually nearly wrecked. Poor Ned. He had his dreams, but he could never translate them into action. He seemed to have an irresistible urge to pull things to pieces, but like "all the King's horses and all the King's men", he never could put them together again. Out of all our homes, we only had one piano, and it happened to be in one of the many houses in which Ned was domi-ciled. We have yet to learn what his vision was for its glo-rious future, but it had an inevitable and ignominious end in a hundred spare parts on some scrap heap. His tortuous mind would always put the blame for his failures on oth-ers, accusing them of a lamentable lack of intelligence. He would then seek solace, and a relief from his woes, in drink. It was the one escape from the haunting reality of his life. Like many thousands more, Ned is the victim of an overpowering sub-conscious urge, over which he has lit-tle or no control. He is a most unhappy man, waging constant warfare against his foe, yet being continually overwhelmed. So often it happens that the despair at his own inadequacy is the cause of defeat, driving his shat-tered "ego" to the solace of the bottle. The "Neds" of this world need us. They need our support and comfort, and above all our understanding and patience. So often in the past, the Christian church has been sadly lacking in these last two essentials. May God give us grace to supplement our prayers by His compassion.

So often either drink or drugs was the dominant factor in bringing men before the courts. My telephone rang one morning just after my arrival at the office. A quiet cultured voice spoke.

"This is Doctor__ I am looking for accommodation."

"I'm sorry," I replied, "but our accommodation is for ex-offenders." The speaker again spoke with a quiet dignity.

"I am an ex-offender," he said.

I was rather taken aback and I arranged for him to meet us. He was a quiet-spoken, friendly man, of about forty years of age. We had no trouble in verifying his credentials. He was a fully-qualified doctor, and had had a practice in a nearby town. He had become addicted to some of the drugs he had prescribed, and had used his qualification to obtain them for himself. The irregularities had been discovered, and he had been brought before the court, and convicted of offences against the Drugs Act. He had not been struck off the Register, but had been barred from prescribing drugs, rendering him unable to continue in practice. It was a tragic waste of a brilliant brain. His patients loved him. In his case there was little excuse, as he must have been well aware of the risks involved, and the potency and peril of the drug. He appeared to make every effort to co-operate, but we soon found, to our dismay, that he was still able by some obscure means to obtain his own particular brand of poison. He was admitted to the drug-addiction unit at All Saints Hospital. It was a sad sight to see such a remarkably able man humbly queuing for his midday meal at the hatch, instead of sitting at the desk in his surgery advising and admonishing us lesser mortals. It emphasised the thraldom to which the victim is subjected, and his pathetic impotence. If such as he cannot free themselves from the abject slavery, with all its attendant misery, how can we hope to liberate the pathetic youngsters who haunt the sleazy dives of the underworld? We have seen so many put up a brave fight, and to their credit be it said, that some have won through. We have seen many die.

Like many more, we have lost touch with Doctor __. Another "ship that has passed in the night", but remains in our mind as another victim of a sinister and implacable foe. Thank God there is One who . . .

Breaks the power of cancelled sin,
And sets the prisoner *free*.

CHAPTER TWELVE

THE LAD WHO LOVED CARS

The night was dark, and the damp, murky haze dimmed the street lights. Billy looked furtively up and down, alert to any sound. All was quiet. He approached the car, a brand-new shiny saloon, and his sensitive fingers caressed it, much as a mother would handle her young child. He gently lifted the bonnet, and after a few moments replaced it. A little deft manipulation of the lock, and he was inside. He soon had the engine purring. By some strange quirk of his mental make-up, Billy always felt safe inside a car. It was his own little cocooned world, and somehow he felt it was part of him. Before he entered the car, it was cold and lifeless, but under the touch of his fingers, it had sprung to life, a living vibrant entity. There was a bond of sympathy and understanding between himself and the car. It responded to his moods.

Almost silently he slipped into gear and the car moved forward. He thought he heard a shout, but he was now completely absorbed in driving slowly, smoothly, through the deserted streets.

It was half an hour later that he first saw the ominous blue light in his mirror, flashing its warning. Billy knew what it meant. He had seen it so often before. Fear gripped him, fear of being parted from his newfound friend, who was responding so loyally to every touch from his hands and feet, fear of being unceremoniously manhandled by the "men in blue", and then the claustrophobic horror of the cell. His foot went down on the accelerator, and the car leapt forward, like a greyhound released from the leash. It seemed to know and understand, and was with him in this. The needle was soon showing 80 mph. It was a built-up area, but the streets were very quiet. Traffic lights at red, and he heard brakes screech behind him, but he was through. His foot was right down now. He saw the island a little too late. He jammed on his brakes, a sickening lurch, a crash, and then the searing agony of broken bones.

They lifted him out, whimpering, not at the excruciating pain of his torn body, but at the twisted mass of steel that had been his friend. He'd killed, killed something that had helped him, and understood him.

I first met Billy towards the end of a three year sentence. He had spent the greater part of his twenty-eight years in penal institutions, and nearly always for taking and driving away cars. The odd thing was, that in nearly every instance, with the exception of the one he crashed, the vehicles were recovered in better condition than when they were stolen. He had a fractured pelvis and femur in the crash, but it had not deterred him. He told me that the only time he felt content and secure was inside a car, with the world shut outside. In some strange way it gave him something that had been denied to him through infancy, childhood, and adolescence, a sense of security and the need to love and be loved. He had been rejected by his parents, and brought up in a children's home. Throughout his formative years he had never known anyone to respond to his warm-hearted, but inarticulate and often incoherent approaches. He had sensed the impatience, and the rejection, of his childish advances, and had slowly withdrawn from all human associations, and instead had lavished his affections on inanimate cars, investing them, in his warped mind, with life and feeling and response. He bestowed on them the care of a parent. He nurtured them, and nursed their ailments. He cleaned and polished, he scrutinised and examined every part, and he was jealously possessive of any vehicle under his care. This was his undoing when he obtained employment at a garage. He had a natural adaptability for the work, and was a good mechanic, but he violently resented anyone else being involved with a car with which he had dealt. It led to altercations, and ultimately to dismissal.

In all his relations with us, Billy appeared to be a very polite young man, almost deferential. We sensed, however, the underlying suspicion with which we were regarded. It was a deep-seated canker at the root of his nature. He identified our friendliest advances with authority, and he hated authority, as it had been translated to him over the years, in approved school, in detention centre, in Borstal, and finally in prison. He had rebelled against it and fought it, and had gone through a great deal of mental torture in the punishment cells, especially on one occasion when he had been encased in a "straightjacket". He had been taught religion in a children's home, but he equated it with the rigid discipline of the institution. Neither the love of God nor of man had been communicated to him in terms of humanity and compassion, nor in a language he could comprehend. He distrusted everyone.

He was a shrewd student of psychology, but his assessments were based on a warped hypothesis.

This was the young man that was brought to us, not too optimistically, by a probation officer some three years ago. Our first problem was to show him that although he did not trust us, we were prepared to trust him. We gave him his own room, and he had access to all the amenities of the house. There were no "dos" and "don'ts". We possessed a small six cwt. van, and we noticed his interest and knew the overpowering urge he would have to get at the wheel. At the same time we knew he had disqualifications which would extend for nearly two years. One day he asked if he could clean the van for me.

"Would you like to buy it?" I asked him. He regarded me quizzically.

"You know I can't drive," he replied.

I sensed his distrust of my motives.

"I'll sell it you for £200," I offered, "and you can pay me each week just as much as you can afford, but on one condition, you'll promise not to drive it until you have a licence. You can strip it down, paint it, clean it, and do as you like with it, anything except drive it."

He gave me his word. At first, he thought he would be watched. I made one or two surreptitious checks on the milometer, and I knew he had been taking the van around the back streets in the early hours of the morning. We made no comment. We soon found that he was trying to convince us that he was keeping his word. We appreciated the risk, but the stakes were high. We were fighting for a man's soul. Soon the mileage recording was stationary. He washed the van, and painted it in an exotic colour scheme. He changed the wheels and did repairs both necessary and unnecessary. He painted his name on it. The van was his own. We began to notice many meaningful little acts of kindness, not to ingratiate himself with us, but just to please us. They were impulsive, but spontaneous, and they were the first indications of a heart responding to care. Surely the ice was melting.

"Do you know," he told us one morning in April, "this is the first time I've seen spring, and the green country, outside prison walls."

We had many problems over the ensuing months, but at Adullam we became accustomed to sitting on the edge of a volcano, hoping and praying that the eruption will not come. We sometimes saw the fissuring, warning us of the lurking forces beneath the seemingly calm crust, waiting to spew out the hot black lava upon our carefully tended soil. It never happened.

The great day arrived at last, when the period of disqualification ended, and Billy was able to apply for a "provisional licence". We saw to it that he had a qualified driver available to accompany him. He was back on the road, and as a responsible citizen, within the law. We arranged for him to have driving lessons with a qualified instructor, and finally, a driving test. He failed, and we feared the worst. We waited for an emotional outburst, but it did not come. He failed again at the second attempt, and again took it philosophically, and with remarkable aplomb. He passed at the third attempt.

Billy left us shortly afterwards, and the last time we saw him, he was driving his own car, an old model which he had bought at a giveaway price, but which we knew he would soon have in working order. It was scrupulously clean, interior and exterior. We would like to hear that he found a life-partner, who would give him the love that life had denied him. Sadly, we have to admit that this is something we cannot provide at Adullam.

We sometimes feel that our caring comes too late. By the time that the love-starved child has struggled through the problems of adolescence, and been thrust out upon a cold uncaring world, the tender conscience has been seared, and irreparable damage done. We surely need a far more militant and understanding Christian church, who will be equipped and able to meet the demands of people like Billy in their early years, and to supplement our "social welfare" with the tender love their hungry hearts require, and yearn for.

CHAPTER THIRTEEN

WHY LEN SLASHED HIS CHEST

I had a friendly chat with most of the patients in the drug addiction unit. Len always seemed to appreciate our bedside talks. He was always an interesting conversationalist, and unlike most would be willing to talk on any topic. The pallor of his thin face was accentuated by a mop of jet black hair. I had noticed a number of thin white lines crisscrossing his chest, but I hesitated to show any curiosity. It was some time before he told me of his early history, and their origin. He came from the south of Ireland, and assured me he was a Catholic, although he appeared to have no present contact with the church.

"I got involved with drugs at thirteen," he explained. "We used to get 'purple hearts', when I was at school and it wasn't long before I was 'drilling'." Len was twenty-six when we met, and the tell-tale punctures were very obvious.

"I suppose you're wondering what these white marks are," he asked me one day quite casually. I confessed my interest.

"I had a good home, and good parents," he went on, after a pause. "I suppose they were bound to find out, sooner or later. I was eighteen when it all came out. I think they'd suspected for some time, but I was pretty good at concealing my craving. I just couldn't afford the stuff by then, and I'd been borrowing from friends of my dad. I had a terrible row with him. He called in the local doctor. He knew his stuff, and was very helpful. He put me on a substitute drug, but it didn't satisfy my craving for heroin. I took some money from my mother's purse, and ran out of the house. I managed to get a shot, but my parents found out, and they ended up by locking my bedroom door. That drove me crazy. I went berserk. I found a razor blade, and I banged and kicked on the door, and told them that if they didn't let me out I'd cut my throat. I started to slash my chest with the blade. My dad opened the door, and I threatened to kill him. My chest was a mass of blood, but I don't remember feeling any pain. They closed and locked the door again, and telephoned for the doctor. He came at once. They opened the door, and I remember seeing him in the doorway. I was just plumb crazy, and I went for him with the razor blade. He must have hit me on the chin, right on the point. I went out like a light. I think he'd done some amateur boxing. They took me to hospital, and I was there for two months."

Most of the youngsters I met in the unit tended to be colourful and dramatic in their accounts of their experiences, but there was the visual evidence on Len's chest, and I never had any reason to doubt his lurid story. He had left home shortly after his discharge from hospital, and came over to England in search of a lucrative job, and a cheaper market for drugs.

He became involved in the London underworld. His ready wit, and above average intelligence were invaluable assets in the struggle for survival. He had quite an attractive personality, and he soon became attached to an equally attractive girl. She was Len's ultimate salvation. Apart from her physical attraction, she had a charming personality, and a strength of character and integrity which provided a strange contrast to Len's inherent weakness, and moral instability. They appeared to be a very ill-assorted pair. Her patience was sorely tried by his often ill-tempered moods, and the perversity of his ways. She knew of his addiction, and stood by him courageously, convinced that it could, and would be conquered. In fairness to Len it must be admitted that he did, at times, make very determined efforts to defeat the habit. This was undoubtedly the reason for his present period in All Saints Hospital. Monica (that is not her real name, for we must preserve her anonymity) visited him on several occasions, journeying from her home town some distance away at her own expense. She was very loyal, and he had little to offer in return. The poison in his system had taken its toll.

After his discharge we were able to find Len accommodation. Like most of his fraternity, he was full of good resolutions, and for a few months they were faithfully kept. Unfortunately, he decided that an occasional drink would be quite permissible. It made a breach in the barriers of resistance, and they were soon broken down. His intake of liquor increased to an unacceptable limit, and in the periods of depression that followed, he was again having recourse to the needle. There was a seemingly masochistic twist to his addiction. At times he would inject the needle with an empty syringe.

We were very discouraged, but Monica was undaunted. With such an example of patient perseverance we dared not give up. She was prepared to sacrifice so much for him. She was very talented, and had sung in opera. Many men would have worshipped at her feet, but everything was laid aside in unstinting devotion to a man addicted to drugs and drink. Foolish? Yes, but how splendid! Her selfless dedication humbled me.

Len was always unpredictable. He seemed to think that this was an attractive facet to his character, but it was the cause of much anxiety to Monica, and added greatly to the burden of his would-be helpers. We seldom knew just where he would be at a given time. It was encouraging to find that his periods of total abstinence were becoming longer, but his lapses always caused concern. On one occasion, he was arrested on a minor charge, and a hypodermic needle and syringe were found on him, but no drugs. He was fined and discharged.

We had lost trace of Len for some weeks. Then a message came from Monica to say that he had taken a bedsitter in Handsworth. She gave the address, and I promised to call. I went the same evening. He was in a small room on the second floor of a rather untidy house. He was in bed, and obviously under the influence of drugs. Monica was with him. His speech was incoherent, and the girl was very distressed. She showed me some small white capsules, and asked what she should do with them. She had found them under his pillow.

"I'll take them," I told her. We found no trace of a syringe, or needle. The years of necessity had made him an adept of concealment. I offered to stay, but Monica assured me that she would prefer to look after him herself. I was a little apprehensive, but I knew she was a capable person, and could handle a crisis. I returned home, telling her to phone me if she needed help.

My telephone rang at about 10 p.m. It was Len's voice, still a little blurred, but his words were slowly and carefully enunciated.

"Mr Moore?" I acknowledged my identity.

"You've got my stuff. I want it back."

"Sorry, Len," I answered, "but you're not getting it."

"Look here," his voice was throaty, and almost a whisper, "you either bring it back, or I'll finish myself off. And you know I mean it."

There were a few moments of silence. I dared not trust myself to speak. I replaced the receiver. I remembered those ominous white lines on his chest . . . and the frenzy of his drug-starved nerves. What if he carried out his threat? . . . Would I be to blame? . . . Would his death be forever searing my conscience? I must either return the drug . . . or face the consequences. My wife was with me in the room.

"Let us take it to the Lord in prayer," she said. We did.

> What a privilege to carry . . .
> Everything to God in prayer.

We rose from our knees reassured, and with a peace in our hearts.

"What are you going to do? She asked.

"Nothing," I replied.

In half an hour the phone rang again. I must admit to some trepidation as I picked it up. At best our faith is weak. It was Monica's voice. It was quite calm and composed.

"I just wanted to tell you that Len's quite all right now."

"Thank God!" I said it with reverence and a full heart.

"He calmed down after a while, and he said to tell you not to worry," Monica explained.

We again went down on our knees, this time with a prayer of thanksgiving. How wonderful it is to have One who never fails us in these times of crisis. My wife and I were both in our middle seventies, and the frequency and repetition of these ordeals would inevitably have ended in a breakdown for one, or even both of us, if we had not been able to cast our burden upon an Almighty God. It was always a help to share these problems with each other, and being human, we so often sought our own solution. Like "Christian" in "Doubting Castle" we often forgot that we had the key in our pockets.

Len, for a time, had become deeply involved with the Messengers, a dedicated group of young people linked with the Sparkbrook Mission. Members of this outreach team had made contact with him at All Saints Hospital during one of their regular visits there. Besides working with addicts, visiting pubs and coffee bars with the gospel, these youngsters also ran Late Night Special, a gospel meeting for all and sundry at Birmingham Parish Church (St. Martin's) each Sunday evening. The meetings were held in the Church Hall after evensong.

The Rector, Canon Bryan Green, had invited all those who took part in Late Night Special to conduct evensong one Sunday, and present this ministry to his regular congregation, most of whom never took part in outreach work.

Len, with several other addicts from All Saints, attended the service, and when the leader of the group, Dan Wooding, preached and then invited those who wished to accept Christ to come forward, Len was the first to the front. That night he made his decision for Christ.

We would have liked to have ended Len's story in the conventional manner, with wedding bells, and an assurance that he and Monica lived happily ever after. With the addict, it seldom ends that way. Monica gave him another two years of devotion, until she was drained emotionally, mentally, and physically. A vital prerequisite of a happy and lasting union must surely be mutual confidence and respect. Len's vulnerability and unpredictable moods had slowly but inexorably taken their toll, and shattered all such illusions. It is sad that in the hour of success they had to separate, but they were quarrelling much too often and they mutually agreed to part.

It is good to know that such sacrificial devotion was not utterly in vain. The last time we saw Len we were amazed at the transformation in his appearance. Gone was the sickly pallor of his face, and the involuntary nervous twitching of the fingers. He was bright-eyed, full of self-assurance, and seemed completely revitalised. He told me that the old habits were conquered and cured. He acknowledged the Divine intervention in his life, but was still young in his faith. He has now found a new partner, and is happily married.

CHAPTER FOURTEEN

THE REBEL WHO FOUND GOD

Whether we prefer to call it crime, or delinquency, or even more euphemistically, anti-social behaviour, it can usually be traced back to childhood, and even to early infancy. Colin had taken more than his share of buffetings as far back as he could remember. There were blurred memories of beatings, nightmarish ordeals of almost unbearable pain, and shivering in sheer terror at the sound of his father's footsteps. He could never quite understand why, but he knew it usually happened at night, when his father came home from the pub up the road. He used to scream at first, but this only seemed to inflame his dad's ill-temper, and he soon learned to silently smother his sobs under the pillow. He was in a hostile world, where nobody seemed to care very much about him, and even his mother was so often strange and unsympathetic. He was terrified of his father, and a little afraid of his mother. His natural need for dependency upon his parents was met by blows and beatings, and his need for love, by a callous indifference.

Colin was the eldest of a family of ten. He remembers bitter quarrels between his parents, and this was reflected in the less-important squabbles between the youngsters. At ten years old, he could not be expected to adopt the role of peacemaker, and it was inevitable that he "took sides", and became involved. It was so often the "law of the jungle", and the survival of the fittest. It was an unhappy home, and he rebelled against its misery, and sought consolation in the larger world outside. His childhood toughened him, and he became an accepted leader among the more unruly members of his own age group. The world was his oyster, to be forcibly prised open.

There were late night excursions to derelict houses, where they learnt the first elementary lessons in the art of "breaking and entering". They would sneak home in the early hours of the morning, and he would creep up the stairs, unobserved on most occasions. Sometimes, however, his father caught him, and there was an unmerciful thrashing with the fist.

At fourteen, Colin decided to leave home. At first it was good fun. He had an occasional meal at the home of one of his friends, and he could always nick the few odd cakes, or a bar of chocolate. He was an innocent looking youngster, and did not arouse the suspicions of friendly shopkeepers. Sleeping was no problem. He knew most of the derelict houses in the area, and he kept well away from the vicinity of his home during the daytime. He knew they would be looking for him, and even if they weren't, the school authorities would soon be on his track. He realised he would need some means of support, and began to look with envious eyes on the tills, and their evidence of untold wealth.

Unfortunately for him, disaster came with his first major enterprise. It was really a well-planned affair, with Colin as the mastermind. The two involved had satisfied themselves that the locality was not patrolled by the "men in blue". The objective was a supermarket, where the rear premises were apparently quite accessible. The plan was that they would carefully remove one or two articles, and store them in their hideout, until a customer could be found.

When Colin and his pal crept furtively and silently up the dark passage, it was about 1 a.m. They managed to force the rather inadequate lock, and gain entrance. Then on the threshold of success came their Nemesis. They had forgotten the burglar alarm. The horrifying strident clanging broke the silence of the night. The two lads panicked and rushed for the door, and found to their consternation that it had automatically closed and locked. They were trapped. It was with a very deflated ego that Colin was escorted to the police station. He knew that worse was to come when he would have to face his father. To his surprise, however, he was not returned to his home. He was brought before the court, where a full report had been given on his background, and instead he was placed "in care".

Conditions at the children's home were quite good, and the amenities were all that the normal child would need. There was, however, a very strict discipline, which Colin, who was now a rebel, found irksome. He was convinced that nobody was on his side, and he had to wage his own war against the world. He could not go out at night to meet the only people who seemed to understand his needs. Three times he absconded, only to have the humiliation of being brought back and punished. His next attempt was better planned. He hitch-hiked as far away

as he could get, and finished at Doncaster. His only chance
of obtaining the necessities of life was by theft, but as he
was not yet adept in the niceties of the "profession" he was
soon caught again, and once more appeared before the
Courts. This time he was sent to an approved school, with
its still more severe discipline and tighter security.

"I just hated it," he told me. "I wanted to be free, free to
do my own thing, and to live my own life. I told some of
the lads there that I was going to make a break for it, but
they thought I hadn't the guts. When the crunch came,
and they knew I meant it, they helped me all they could. I
slipped out quietly one night. I knew it would give me a
few hours start before I was missed. I managed to 'hitch-
hike' again, in a lorry, and by daybreak I was up north.
This time I managed to get a job as an apprentice chef.
They were a mixed bunch at the hotel, and I suppose I was
as bad as any of them. It was then that I had my first taste
of liquor. I acquired a liking for the cheap, rough cider. It
was strong enough to make me want to fight. I had
learned to defend myself against any assault, either real
or imaginary. I wasn't quarrelsome, but I was always
ready for a 'scrap'. I soon found myself 'sacked', and with
nowhere to go."

Colin's pattern of life had by now become established,
and further offences followed, until the "long arm of the
law" again caught up with him. He was re-arrested, and
returned to the approved school, only to abscond again.
He stole a motor-scooter, and this was followed by two
more burglaries, before he was again finally apprehended.
This time, despite pleas for mitigation on account of his
youth, he was sent to the more adequate security of
borstal.

Restrictions were severe, but the company was congenial. They were all rebels like himself, ready to defy and flout all authority. At this stage Colin's rebellion was only verbal. He did not yet have the confidence or the courage to openly show his contempt, and he managed to get through his sentence without incurring any further punishment. On his discharge he returned to the family home to find that his parents had been divorced. His father had left home.

"I was relieved to find he'd gone," he told me. "My mother said that as I was the eldest, I must now take his place. I think she wanted me to keep the kids in order, but I wasn't often around. I had frequent quarrels with Mother, and once when I'd come home drunk we had a real set-to, and I pulled a knife on her. I think after that she was a bit frightened of me. She thought I was taking after my Dad.

"My younger brother was now giving trouble as well. I found out that he'd broken into a house, and among other things, he'd taken a family allowance book. I tried to cash it. I was a bit of a mug in those days. It was a daft thing to do. They arrested both of us. The kid was put on probation, but of course I got sent back to borstal.

"It was the same routine, but I was now a real rebel, and determined to show the authorities that they couldn't push me around any longer. I also wanted to show the other lads that I could 'take it'. No longer satisfied with petty acts of insubordination, I refused point blank to perform the tasks allotted to me. I challenged the staff to try and make me. I did everything within my power to annoy and irritate. Of course, I ended up in the 'punishment block'. In fact I spent most of my time there. We drift into gangs in these places,

according to the type of offence you're in for, and I was
regarded as the leader of our mob. A few spells in the punishment block gives you prestige. They gave us different
coloured ties, according to the length of time you had to
stay there. You started with a blue tie, and then red when
you'd served about half your time. Then before discharge
you got a bronze. My tie never changed. It was always
blue. However, they couldn't keep me there for ever, and
at last I had my discharge. I came out with determination
to live my own life, to take what I wanted, how I wanted,
but to do the job efficiently and professionally. I thought
I'd learned quite a bit 'inside'! How to leave a 'job' without
any fingerprints, and without any evidence. How to silence
all opposition, quickly and silently. I would be a craftsman
at my 'trade'. I did not go back to my family. If I could not
find a comfortable 'pad', I was always prepared to do a bit
of skippering in some empty property."

By now, Colin had really embarked on a career of crime.
There were a series of burglaries, and again he was
brought before the court. He was placed on probation by
a lenient Judge, with a condition of residence at an
approved hostel. He absconded, and was once again on
the run. Eventually caught and arrested, after another
series of "break-ins", he was sentenced to 2½ years.

On his release, nearly two years later, he committed the
unpardonable crime of a violent assault on a policeman.
This time he received a three year sentence.

I asked Colin if his periods in prison had helped him in
any way.

"I don't think so," he replied. "All the time I was in, I
was thinking about how I could become a better burglar,
and how I could get on to the 'big-time' stuff. I hadn't yet

learnt that I was beating my head against a brick wall. I thought I could beat the lot."

It was a depressing story as he continued. I found it hard to reconcile the clear-eyed friendly fellow in front of me, with the man he described.

"You soon get mixed up with gangs," he went on. "I was with a crowd of about twenty. We called ourselves the AB & C gang, probably for want of something better. We used to specialise in nicking TV sets and stereos from shops. It's easier working with a gang. You're better organised, and you've always got the area patrolled. We know who's about. Of course the real problem is to get rid of the stuff, but you get to know the reliable 'fences'. They're a crafty lot, and they can put the screw on you if they want to. I got picked up again, but jumped my bail, and was once more on the run. We carried on with a few more 'smash and grabs', and I thought I was getting pretty smart in eluding arrest. There were rival gangs of course, and we got into a bit of bother with one of them. We had a real set-to in one of the pubs. One of my mates got badly beaten-up, and we decided to go after them."

I'd heard of gang warfare, but Colin's lurid account of what followed brought it home to me in all its sordid and stark realism.

"I took a pick axe handle from a building site," he told me. "We all had something. They had nicked a car, and we waylaid it up a side street. We made 'em pull up, and then 'went in'. I remember smashing the windows of the car with my handle, and letting them have it. One of them was a good bit older than the rest, a big burly fellow. I hit him hard, I'll never forget the crunch as my handle hit his skull. He went out like a light. I saw the blood pouring out, and I thought I'd better get clear. I ran hard, and I managed to get away, but I was picked up two days later. The police arrested twenty-two of us. I knew it would be 'curtains' for me this time. I was sent to Crown Court.

"I had a nasty shock when my turn came. The Judge was the same chap that had previously sentenced me, and he'd been very lenient then. He gave me a cold look. Even then I was not prepared for the extreme severity of his sentence. Two years for the 'grievous bodily harm', and one year for 'jumping' my bail, the sentences to run consecutively. Three years, three more years of misery, of punishment cells, of being pushed around, of being told what to do, and being made to do it. For the first time I was beginning to think that I was losing the battle. The rebellion was still there, but some of the old cock-sureness was beginning to go. I was starting to wonder just where I was missing out on life."

Colin did not tell us much about his period of imprisonment, which lasted for over two years. It must have been a time for reflection and re-assessment, and some deep thinking. He was now in his early twenties, and the major portion of his life had been spent in some sort of institution. His mother had now remarried, and this accentuated the estrangement between himself and his family. He had no desire to renew any relationship with his father. The only person for whom he had any real respect and affection was his grandmother, a sincere Christian lady, who had always given him a welcome at her home. She was very concerned for him, and was constant in her prayers on his behalf.

"She always preached at me," he told me, ruefully. "I always got a lecture when I visited her, but she was always kind, and she was the one person who really seemed to care what happened to me."

Colin went to her on his release on parole, but she could only give him temporary accommodation, and he was faced with the ever recurring problem of where to live. He had an ingrained dislike of hostels, with their list of rules, and rigid meal times. It savoured too much of the repression of his past life. He felt that they were only one remove from borstal and jail. It was natural that he should visit some of the old haunts, and meet his old companions, and it may have been to his ultimate benefit that he was arrested for a burglary he did not commit. It was the hand of the Almighty delivering him from further involvement with the criminal elements with which he had so long been associated. Stirring somewhere in the mystic depths of his soul was a new hunger, a cry for release, inarticulate but insistent. He felt he could not face another stretch of imprisonment. He was resentful at the injustice of his arrest, but for the first time he really felt afraid. He was released on bail, his sister standing as surety for him, and he returned to his grandmother's home.

"She started to preach again," he told me, "but somehow this time it seemed different. I listened and her words began to sink in. She told me to start to read the Bible, and I asked her if she could get me one. The next time I went to see her she had got one for me. I didn't understand much at first, but I really did read it."

I remembered my own experience, and my brother-in-law's persistence and importunity, in urging me to seek God. How thankful must we be for the saints who persevere in prayer for us, in the face of rejection and ridicule.

Colin was discharged and finally released. Granny was relieved, and immediately contacted the probation service at Perry Barr, Birmingham in the hope of finding him a safer haven.

The probation service got in touch with us, and we met Colin for the first time. We sensed his antagonism to the hostel atmosphere, but managed to convince him that we were rather different, and he agreed to join us. Neither he nor his grandmother realised at first that we were a Christian organisation, and he seemed surprised when our other Colin told him of our faith. God indeed was moving "in a mysterious way, His wonders to perform". There was no sudden or emotional surrender. Colin continued to read his Bible, and the Holy Spirit was quietly opening the blind eyes of his soul. Christ had entered into his life as surely as He entered the virgin's womb. A new creature was born.

It is hard for us to reconcile the person he told us about with the man we know today. It is indeed a miracle of grace, at which we stand amazed.

It was not long before we asked him to join our staff. We were opening a small hostel as an assessment centre, to assist us to place our new people in the right type of house, and the right environment. It was an important step forward, and Colin was ideally suited to take charge. He knew and understood the pressures and anxieties of the man just released from prison. He was a shrewd judge of a man's character, and could sift the wheat from the chaff. Colin soon became an integral part of our organisation. His story illustrates the terrifying consequences of the lack of parental care and discipline, but thankfully, in Colin's case, of the triumph of redeeming grace.

CHAPTER FIFTEEN

"IT'S FOR MURDER, MUM"

They were a very ordinary family living very ordinary lives in a back street of a northern town. Dad liked his pint at the "local", but seldom got drunk. Mum kept a keen eye on the household economy, and on Dad's wage packet. There were three rather boisterous children at home, two girls age seven and nine, and Bob, a boy of fourteen. There was, of course, nineteen-year-old Jim, a paratrooper in the RAF, who came home periodically on leave, and Jim's girl-friend, Pam, who sometimes made the 800 miles round journey from the south of England to visit them. She was one of the family now. Jim was young Bob's idol, the object of his hero worship, and he never tired of telling his pals lurid tales about Jim's parachute "drops", elaborated and embellished by his own lively imagination. Dad was very proud of Jim. He loved to talk about "my lad wi' the paras". They were a happy family.

Jim and Pam were to be married in two months' time. The preparations were well ahead, and special leave had been granted to Jim for the wedding. Jim's family and friends were more numerous than that of Pam's, so it was mutually agreed that the wedding should take place in

Northumberland, and not at the bride's home in Devon. It was, of course, a break with tradition, but it was generally accepted that it would be far more economical and convenient. The couple would then go down south, nearer to Jim's depot, for a brief honeymoon.

The telephone call came late in the evening. A neighbour, some three doors away, who had a telephone, tapped at the door. Dad opened it.

"Is that you, Joe? Your Pam's on the phone, would you come, she sounds a bit upset."

"See what she wants, Dad," shouted Mum, from the kitchen. "If they've 'ad a row she shouldn't be bothering us at this time o' night. Tell 'er to sort it out themselves. Sorry you've been bothered, Mrs. K."

Mum usually took command. Dad put his slippers on and went out. He returned ten minutes later. His face seemed slightly distorted, and his fingers were twitching nervously. Mum was finishing ironing a shirt. She hadn't seen his face.

"Well, and what's up now? Has she chucked 'im up again, has she . . .?"

The old man's voice was almost a croak.

"Mum, they've got Jim . . ." The words seemed to choke him.

"Got Jim, what yer mean?" She turned round and saw the agony in his eyes. He was like a stricken child.

"They've arrested 'im."

"Arrested 'im? What for? 'E's bin driving that car again, that's wot."

"No, Mum."

"Then what's the silly young fool bin doin'?"

Dad's voice had gone. It was nearly a whisper.

"It's for murder, Mum . . ."

Dad's story was very confused, and it was some time before they could piece it together. It seemed that Jim had been returning from a dance rather late, and had thumbed a passing car. They had pulled up in a lay-by, and for what seemed at the time no apparent reason, there had been a quarrel, and the driver had been battered to death. To make matters worse, Jim had driven off in the car, which was later found abandoned. It was a grim and sordid story.

The trial was in Birmingham some three months later. The probation service asked us to accommodate Jim's father and mother, and Pam, for the duration of the proceedings, and it so happened that one of our houses was available.

The girl seemed to be suffering the most, although it is hard to assess the depths of anguish in the inmost soul. The father was numbed and very confused, and seemed unable to take it all in. None of them could relate the young man they all knew with the brutal and callous crime. Surely, somewhere along the line, there had been some ghastly mistake in identity. It just couldn't have been Jim – happy, carefree, lovable Jim. It was just a terrible nightmare from which they must surely awake. Their minds just couldn't accept the gross and gruesome horror of it all.

The court proceedings lasted for four long, agonising days. We knew the futility of any words of ours to offer comfort, or ease the tension, but we invited the family to join us in our little sanctuary, our "upper room", which we had for so long dedicated to daily evening worship in our home. Many had been the problems and heartaches of

people of all ages that had been poured out here, at the
throne of grace. Youngsters still in their teens, in the merciless grip of drugs; older men driven to the verge of
despair by drink; all with their tales of broken homes, broken lives, broken promises; somehow they seemed to be
able to draw near to God in this "upper room". Maybe the
daily prayers of nearly thirty years had given it an aura of
sanctity. I do not know. The mother and Pam came along,
and it was here that we sought the comfort and peace of
the only One who can mend a broken heart. Pam really
emptied her soul before the Lord, and poured out her grief.
In the surge of sorrow which had well-nigh overwhelmed
her, she found a wonderful inward peace which seemed to
sustain her through her long ordeal. She acquired strength
which enabled her to support the stricken parents. She was
very much in love, and her suffering was intense, but she
now had a courage and fortitude beyond our expectations.
I was thankful that my wife was with me, with the tender
compassion that only a woman can give. It was a gruelling
experience for all of us.

It was an exceptionally busy week, and I could not
attend all the court proceedings, but Pam asked me to be
with her on the final day of the trial. I knew that in the face
of damning evidence she still hoped for an acquittal. She
still clung to her faith in Jim and as I looked at the young
fellow in the dock, fresh-complexioned, clear-eyed and
erect, one wondered at the sheer incongruity of it all. He
occasionally glanced round, as if to assure himself of her
presence, and on one occasion their eyes met, and he gave
a friendly smile.

The Judge was giving his summing-up. The drama
was tense, and almost unreal. We were just waiting for the

curtain to fall, and then we would be back again to reality. It was like a macabre charade, a performance of puppets, each one pirouetting at the pulling of some hidden wire.

He had finished, and the Judge and jury retired. There was now a subdued chatter among the court officials, their faces impassive and unemotional. I glanced at Pam. She was rigid and dry-eyed, and deathly white. The mother was dabbing her eyes. There was a momentary hush, and the jury filed in.

We all stood as the Judge entered and took his seat, his face a mask of expressionless austerity.

"Are you all agreed on your verdict?"

"Yes, my Lord."

"Do you find the defendant guilty or not guilty?"

"Guilty, my Lord."

I felt Pam slump against me. Nature had brought relief at last. She was unconscious for a short period, but soon recovered. Her eyes were dry, and it was she who comforted the weeping mother. She took control with an efficiency and maturity far beyond her years as they left the court.

With the help of a welfare officer at the jail, I was able to see Jim on the following day. He was in solitary confinement, as is usual for a period after a life sentence. He was quite composed, and did not seem unduly distressed, but as the interview had to be in the presence of prison officers, I had little opportunity of assessing his reactions. He was allowed a short meeting with Pam. She was very brave, and this time it was he who broke down. He begged her to stand by him through the bleak years ahead, and she promised that she would.

We have lost touch with the family, but Pam has written to us, and asked us to continue in prayer for her. She visits

Jim as often as circumstances allow. She has accepted a renunciation of so much that life has to offer, on the altar of her love, but with a faith that has been strengthened and enriched. To me, it was one of the most harrowing situations that I had been called upon to face. Our hearts went out to the girl and the stricken family.

Only those in close touch can know the poignancy and the pity of it, and the sheer hell, with all its humiliation and shame, the averted glances of folk who once welcomed you, and maybe even worse, the pity of people who respected you. Yes, they were just ordinary folk, like you and me, living ordinary lives, until the whole world erupted around them. It could never be the same again. The lad they once knew and loved was dead, and yet somehow lived, a gruesome spectre that could not, and would not be exorcised. We need to know the One who "comforteth us in all our tribulation, that we may be able to comfort them which are in any trouble, by the comfort with which we ourselves are comforted of God" (2 Corinthians 1:4).

How pitifully inept and inadequate we are in such circumstances, until Christ himself speaks in us and through us by the Holy Spirit, a living message of hope to hearts from which all hope has gone. To people like Pam, to the broken-hearted parents, and yes, by God's grace and his infinite mercy, to Jim.

CHAPTER SIXTEEN

MERSEY BOUND

It seemed the natural outcome of our success in Birmingham that we should extend our horizons, and our contacts with Liverpool appeared to indicate Merseyside as our next venture. We were in touch with the local probation service, and they were very encouraging, and offered us every help and co-operation. We were always frequent visitors at Salem, the church in Belvedere Road where I had made my first commitment to Christ. They had an energetic and enthusiastic group of young people who had always taken an active interest in our work, and they readily consented to take on the responsibility of the new enterprise. Peter Wildman, a teacher in religious studies at one of the local schools, agreed to pioneer the work, initially on a voluntary basis, and later to make it his full time career. He had an academic qualification for his scholastic work, and also the security which is incidental to the profession, but although he had the responsibility of a wife and young family, he did not hesitate in making his decision. We were very grateful for this, as he had a natural adaptability for the type of work involved, with his extrovert disposition and easy-going camaraderie with all and sundry, and a total commitment to Christian work. Whoever crossed the threshold of his home could not but sense the warmth, and uninhibited welcome within. Whatever your social standing or background, you were always at ease, with both Peter and his attractive young wife, Dorothy. It was always Pete and Dot, and, of course, there were the four boisterous youngsters, two of whom had been adopted. It was a happy home, and a fine example to the many of society's misfits, whom he would often invite in for a meal and a chat.

Within months, we had a nucleus of three homes, thanks to the efforts of the probation service, and the sympathetic interest of Liverpool's largest housing association Merseyside Improved Houses. It soon became necessary for Peter to leave the school, and give his whole time to the work. We were building on the same basic concepts and principles as at Birmingham, providing homes where our people could live independently, and establish their own way of life. More by accident than by design we found that we were dealing with a younger age group, but their ebullience was countered by the enthusiasm of Peter and his group of young volunteers, most of whom were on the right side of thirty.

Brian was one of our earliest residents. He was brought to us by a probation officer shortly after the opening of our first home. He was under voluntary "after-care". He had no established home, and though still in his twenties, he had quite a formidable record. He was a rather pale faced young man, slightly built, and at first appeared withdrawn and uncommunicative, but the friendly atmosphere of the home soon broke down his reserve, and he became co-operative, and anxious to help. He came along to the church service without any undue pressure, and

soon became a regular visitor to Salem. Brian related to us
something of his early life. He was a native of the Black
Country town of Walsall, in Staffordshire.

"My mother died of tuberculosis when I was seven," he
told us. "We were all packed off to the isolation hospital,
and my young brother died of the complaint. He was only
six months old. It was a deadly disease in those days. I
suppose I must have missed Mother, but things seemed to
happen so suddenly, and I didn't realise that at the time.
After I came out of hospital, they sent me to live with my
grandparents."

I asked Brian about his relationship with his grandparents.

"I never liked my grandfather," he replied. "He was ter-
ribly strict, and a very religious man. Grandma was good
to us in her way, but it was not like being at home, and she
never seemed to understand me. I could never really confide in her, although maybe it was my fault. I was sent to
a comprehensive school and I suppose I got in with the
'bad boys'. When I was fourteen, my grandfather died,
and my father, who used to see us fairly often, was taken
to hospital with our family scourge, TB. I was left to my
own devices after that and I suppose I felt like nobody
cared very much, so nothing mattered. I began to nick
small items, sweets, and anything which seemed handy,
and I got away with it for a long time. It seemed so easy."

Brian later found that it was not always "so easy". The
Law caught up with him, and he was brought before
the courts on a charge of theft. It was Grandma who felt
the real impact of the indignity and disgrace. Brian was
put on probation, which did not seem to upset him much.
Before long he was involved with local gangs of youths,

whose speciality was taking and driving away cars, and disposing of any contents of value. Brian did not yet appreciate the efficiency of the police, and their astuteness in detection. He was arrested again, and this time he was sent to borstal. It was his first experience of compulsory detention, but he said conditions were not bad.

"It was like being at camp," he said, "except that it was a bit more strict. You had to do as you were told, but if you didn't 'play up' it wasn't too hard".

Brian was now eighteen, and had done little or nothing towards finding a job, and a career. He was still associating with the more unruly elements in the town, and was very conscious of the resentment of his grandmother, and his unpopularity in the only home he knew.

"Were there no girlfriends?" I asked him. I could see his hesitation, and I was sorry I had put the question when he rather reluctantly answered.

"Yes, there was one. I was very fond of her." Rather disjointedly, he told me the story of the one real tragedy in his life.

There had been a late night party at a local youth club. It had been boisterous and high-spirited, but there had been no trouble. A number of the young folk had gathered outside the building in animated discussion. It was on a steep hill, and the car park was at the top of the incline. Several cars had already drifted slowly down the hill, but Brian was still with a group outside the building.

It all happened so quickly. They heard a warning shout, and then they saw the car rolling backwards, gathering speed. They thought it was just another prank by some of the wilder ones, and they leapt aside with a shout and a laugh. Then Brian saw her standing in the car's track, suddenly petrified, but he was too late and he had no time to dash across to push her out of the way. A scream, and a sickening thud, and it was all over. He saw her lying there, her white party dress blotched with crimson. There was no response as he bent over her, her face covered in blood.

They took her to hospital, but she was dead on arrival.

Brian was overwhelmed by the shock. He could only give me a hazy account of the cause of the accident, but he understood it was due to a failure of the brakes. There were no criminal proceedings. On a sudden impulse, he decided to enlist in the Army Catering Corps, and signed on for three years. He did not tell us much about this period in his life, but it seems they were comparatively uneventful years during which he kept out of trouble. He had the option of a further three years, but he declined, and was discharged.

Brian returned to Walsall without much prospect of work, and before long he became involved once more in burglaries and theft, with its inevitable consequence. He was again arrested. The court was lenient, and he received a suspended sentence. He realised the implication of this, should he again come before the court, and he decided to move away from the district, this time to Stoke-on-Trent, where he eventually found himself a job in the pits. It was hard work, and he was never too robust, but he persevered for some months, then he decided to move to Liverpool. Here he managed to eke out a precarious living, alternating between odd jobs, and assistance from social security. He stayed at a lodging house where he was reasonably comfortable, until a man arrived with whom he had had contact in Borstal. There was apparently a quarrel, after which Brian left, and was for a time homeless.

He slipped back into the old unhappy ways, and was involved in several burglaries. The tell-tale finger-prints were his undoing. Yet again he had to face the austerity of the court-room, and this time he was sent to Crown Court, and given a two-year sentence. While in jail, he was involved in a conspiracy charge, aiding and abetting in an escape attempt. For this he received a further twelve months, and even with the normal remission, he had to spend well over two years "inside".

It was on his release after the last sentence that we made our first contact with him. The fallow ground had been prepared and ploughed and harrowed by the iron teeth of adversity, and the seeds were sown. Brian soon knew and appreciated the warmth of Christian companionship, and a more congenial environment. Life began to take on a definite pattern, and to have an ultimate purpose, and he responded to the call of an everlasting love. We all noticed the change, as a new creature was born.

As mentioned earlier, it is always difficult to assess a man's motivation, and his aptitude and adaptability for a given environment in an interview. We needed a short stay emergency house, where we could arrange temporary accommodation to meet urgent and immediate needs, and where we could have more opportunity to gauge a man's reactions, before allocating him to any of our homes. A suitable house was made available, and who better than Brian to take over the responsibility of running it? He had the offer of a job, but he readily agreed to join our staff, and he indeed proved a valuable asset. The hard school in which he had been trained, was a far more fitting preparation for the work ahead, than a course in sociology or psychology. We arranged a short stay at a Bible college in

Peterhead, in Scotland, but his inside knowledge of the many pitfalls was his greatest asset, and we soon had him established as the first warden of our Emergency Hostel.

Merseyside has an urgent need, with its labyrinths of back streets, and decaying buildings, its high unemployment, and ever increasing crime rate. We want an acceptable alternative to the prison sentence for so many "first offenders" who are rootless and homeless. The probation services are under ever-mounting pressures, wrestling with yet greater volumes of "social enquiry reports", and they, in their turn, are always seeking suitable accommodation for people under their care. We want homes where the rebel has no need to rebel, and no cause to demonstrate his independence, but where we can keep an unobtrusive but watchful eye on his ways. We need drastic action to relieve our over-crowded prisons, and to combat and stem the rising tide in juvenile delinquency. We need the help and co-operation of the Christian church, and men and women who are willing to become personally involved in the lives of the lost and lonely. Brian's story could be repeated a thousand times, with minor variations. "Come over into Macedonia and help us . . .".

We owe so much of what we have accomplished to the active support of Salem church, and their willing band of volunteers, and also to the co-operation of the Liverpool City Mission, but we need yet more and more as the days bring their ever lengthening tale of broken lives.

CHAPTER SEVENTEEN

SET ME FREE

Most students of juvenile delinquency, or criminology, will strive to find a common denominator in every case history, and in triumph present their statistics to the psychologist and the psychiatrist, and say "Here we have the key to the problem". We confess that we have also made similar attempts, and failed. There is one feature however which occurs with disconcerting frequency in so many of our "social enquiry reports". It is the incidence of the inadequate home background, and the lack of parental control. The resilience of youth will surmount the privations of poverty. They may be ill-fed, ill-clothed and lacking so many of the amenities of life. They may be ill-treated, and still survive to become good law-abiding citizens. Deprive a child of the personal care of his or her parents, however ill-fitted those parents may be for their responsibility, and the shock of finding itself unwanted is too shattering for the young mind to accept. Maybe they will be placed "in care", where all their material needs will be adequately supplied, but nevertheless it will be borne in upon their immature minds that they just don't "belong", that in the final analysis nobody really cares. There is no substitute for home, and Dad and Mum. The children's home is very efficient, and usually staffed by sincere and caring people, but they can never be a real alternative to the security of the family circle, and Mum's good-night kiss.

We knew a family of four that had been placed "in care". Their ages ranged from two to ten. The home was verminous, the children had been sleeping on the floor, with a few dirty coats for covering. The gas had been turned off, due to non-payment of accounts. The father was a heavy drinker, and had a bad record. Nevertheless, when the mother visited the children in the home, it was a heartrending sight to see the younger ones clinging frantically to her, and crying "Don't leave us again, Mum", and the forcible separation as they were dragged screaming from their mother's arms.

"They'll be better off 'in care'," is the usual smug comment. Yes, they'll be better fed, better clothed, bathed and taught the niceties of life, and educated to acceptable standards of behaviour, but the one element to satisfy the child's heart hunger is no longer there, and their love wilts and dies like a flower transplanted into dry and unsuitable soil. The whole plant becomes warped and stultified, a travesty of what might have been.

When all else has failed, there are yet vast untapped sources of mother-love. The foster parent is vastly preferable to the institution. There must obviously be a certain amount of control and supervision, but let it be done by those who have known the meaning of motherhood, rather than by a young bureaucratic martinet, or the well-trained but impersonal social worker. What is the attitude of the Christian church? Are we too fettered and hamstrung by legislation?

There are, of course, so many loveless homes which are fertile breeding grounds for delinquency, but we still feel that our most difficult and intractable cases are from institutions, the so-called "children's homes". We thank God for the exceptions, and the devotion and care which have been bestowed by some of the warm-hearted folk who staff them, but we must always remember that the child needs to "belong", and to feel itself wanted for itself alone. The farmyard hen, with its own nest in the hayloft, scratching for itself, is a happier bird than the battery hen. When these young folk come to us, after graduating from children's home to an approved school, and from there to a detention centre, borstal or prison, the damage is deeply rooted, and the wounds festering.

Discipline is an essential element of mother love. I am not ashamed to admit that my rather limited knowledge of psychology has been based on the word of God. Surely the Creator of the human mind, with its vast ramifications, is the only One to ultimately reveal its hidden depths. The humanist will insist on the inherent goodness of man, but God tells us that the human heart is "deceitful and desperately wicked", and that we are "born in sin, and shapen in iniquity", and in my own case it needs but little introspection to confirm the wisdom and truth of these solemn words, as we probe "the deep and hidden springs, the motives that control". In the early formative years of the child's life, the clay is pliable and soft, and amenable to the deft hand of the potter, but if the shaping is by unskilled, insensitive hands, the hardening soon takes place, and rectification and adjustment becomes more difficult as the years slip by, and the treatment must of necessity be more drastic and severe.

The child's self-interest and urge for self-satisfaction must be controlled, and where there is flagrant flouting of the basic laws of human relationship, there must be correction, and if needed, there must be adequate punishment. It is in the child's own interest, and in the interest of his fellows, that he should learn that any contravention of these laws must be punished. To one child, a sharp word is all that is needed. To another, a few hard slaps on the "backside" will provide a reminder of his obligations. It is usually helpful if a short period elapses between the "sentence" and the administration of the punishment. In my own childhood, this method was always observed, giving me time for reflection, and the contemplation of the pain to follow. There was always the certainty that the sentence would be duly carried out, and very efficiently. There began to be a well-defined relationship between the misdemeanour, and the pain which followed, and my dormant conscience was stirred by the implications of this relationship. I found that "crime did not pay". Sooner or later this lesson must be driven home, as harsher punitive measures become necessary. The sudden impatient slap or blow from an exasperated parent or teacher is always apt to undermine their authority. The child relates it to its own ill-temper, and interprets it as an act of revenge, rather than one of judicial punishment. Justice must be seen to be impartial and impersonal, and never an impulsive reaction of resentment or retaliation. On the other side of the coin, the over-indulgent parent, who hesitates to administer any form of punishment, is failing in the duty of parental love and care. The child who "gets away with it" too frequently and too well, will soon find that his unbridled impulses will ultimately overcome any curbs of his young conscience. The courts receive the "end product" of both camps. They deal with the adolescents and young men who have never been taught the basic tenets of Christianity or ethics. They have never learnt that self-indulgence at the cost or hurt of others must bring retribution, and must ultimately be paid for by themselves. It is a fundamental law of God, and the basic essential of the whole structure of society. It is amazing how so many misguided folk, both in the church and outside of it, tend to undermine this law by the advocacy of the abolition of all the severer types of punishment. They urge the outlawing of all forms of corporal punishment, both for the child and the adolescent, and would turn our "houses of correction", our detention centres, borstals and prisons, into cosy, friendly institutions, with all the social amenities lavishly provided, and where a "good time can be had by all".

At Adullam we believe in the all-embracing, all-conquering power of love. We believe that we should take with meekness and without resentment all that man, at his worst, can hurl at us. We believe that we must forgive again and again and again, until "seventy times seven". The word revenge must never be in our vocabulary, whether it be by invoking the law, or any form of sanctions. We do, however, sincerely believe in God's law, and in man's law, where it is grounded on the same fundamental principles, and also in its adequate administration.

We do not suggest harsher sentences for all and sundry. Justice must be tempered with mercy, and in our splendid judicial system we have very competent Judges who are men of mercy. We do believe, however, that every opportunity should be given for the punishment to fit the crime, and if severity is needed, the hands of justice should not be tied by sentimental, if well-meaning "do-gooders", who would thwart the retribution of evil by their ill-conceived restrictions. We would not advocate the re-introduction of the "cat" but a more humane form of corporal punishment for the young offender, as an ultimate sanction, would undoubtedly act as a deterrent to some of our more unscrupulous young thugs. Let us never be accused of brutality in our prisons but if the rehabilitation of the criminal is our ultimate objective, then let us make the discipline so severe, that after a short sentence they will always fear to return.

There may appear to be a contradiction between our concept of Christian love and forgiveness, and our insistence upon the punishment of the wrongdoer. As professing Christians, we must accept the teaching of the Sermon on the Mount as our standard of behaviour, and it is only by the grace of God that we can attain to the ultimate splendour of its example. To the non-Christian, however, its ideology is illogical, and its standards unattainable. It cannot be applicable to the non-Christian world.

The Sermon on the Mount is a measuring line by which we as Christians are judged, and the world will readily tell us how miserably we fail to meet its requirements. Peter's aggressive attempt to defend his Lord was followed by his denial, with oaths and curses, but he went on to know the completed work of grace, so let us not be discouraged. We have often failed to achieve the standard, and have fallen short of the Master's glorious example of self-denying love, but we learn our lessons, and press forward, with patience and perseverance, until lives are changed, and souls are won. As long as the world rejects Christ, however, the basic principles of the Mosaic law must be applied, if we are to preserve an ordered way of life. Divine love demands the ultimate elimination of evil, and the correction and punishment of the evil-doer.

We do not like classification, with its attendant labels. We speak of the ex-offender, the drug-addict and the alcoholic, and somehow the terms seem to stick. We have to remember that they are just ordinary folk like ourselves, with the same emotions, the same joys, and the same heartaches. Time, circumstance and heredity may have all combined to increase their vulnerability to the temptations of life. Most of us have some inherent weakness, which may be apparent to the world, or concealed like a festering sore beneath the clothing. So often do we have to humbly admit that if we had been called upon to face a similar circumstance such as we read of in a case history, we may have fared worse. We remember Jim, his nervous system shattered by the shock of his mother's death, and the reaction showing itself in the tremors of his hand. We recall his anxiety over it, when seizing on what appeared to be a cure, he found himself enslaved by the drug. We remember Ben, his father dying a drunkard's death and his mother dying shortly afterwards, unloved and unwanted, his only place of welcome the pub. Should we have done better? A really serious and honest answer will no doubt undermine our smug self-satisfaction. These are not isolated cases. They are typical of many. We have tried to focus the attention of the church on their need. "We'll pray for him" says one, and probably the Levite said the same as he went on his way, passing by on the other side. "I couldn't ask him in" says another. "You see I've got young children," and also passes by, leaving him bleeding and helpless. By all means let us pray, but never let prayer be

a substitute for action if we have the power to help. So
often did our Lord meet the physical need, before the more
crucial need of the soul.

There is always a stigma after a prison sentence. It can
seldom be concealed. It is an affront to one's dignity and
self-respect, and undermines any confidence one may have
had in the person concerned. The same stigma will often
pursue them if they move out of their immediate environment into another area, and they find that they are socially
unacceptable. Some are acutely sensitive to the estrangement and ostracism, while some are hardened and indif-
ferent. In either case, it tends to limit their friendships and
associations, and confines them to company less discrimi-
natory. We need to accept them into the church, but the first
stepping stone is an invitation into our own family circle,
not with tolerance and suspicion, but as a welcome guest.
We have never known of any advantage being taken of
such an invitation. Our own home has for many years been
"open house" to many who have been convicted of all
types of crime, including theft, and we have never missed
the smallest item. It has so often been the Open Sesame to
hearts which have been bolted and barred against any sort
of friendship. They need the reassurance of *our* confidence,
they need to be shown that we believe in them, although
they may not believe in themselves.

"I couldn't invite them into my home," I was told by a
Christian friend. "You see there are some very valuable
articles in my room, and it would be placing temptation in
their way." That is the attitude of the world, and it is
understandable, and can be appreciated, but can we, as
followers of Christ, rationalise such an excuse? Are we
prepared to jeopardise our worldly treasure to save a

man's soul? Surely the risk is minimal, the opportunity an open door, and the ultimate goal immeasurable and glorious, the redemption of a soul. We have seen lives transformed, the broken "earthenware" re-fashioned and re-made, because someone with compassion in their hearts invited a lonely man, unwanted and unlovable, into their hearth and home.

If you want to tell them "Please do not smoke here" or "Would you mind wiping your feet on the mat?" . . . it is better not to ask them in. They will probably need a cigarette to put them at ease, and they will be very self-conscious about their muddy shoes. Conversation may at first be difficult, and you will need tact and understanding in finding a topic of sufficient interest to draw them out of their shell. Encourage them to talk, and then be a good listener. Try to be humble in their company. Condescension, however much we try to conceal it, will somehow seep through the veneer. Remember that they will probably be more shrewd in their assessment of yourself, than you will be of them.

Tim had come to us from borstal. His offences had always been "taking and driving away" cars of all types and colours. He just couldn't resist them. He was a friendly lad, and settled in well. We introduced him to a friend who was sympathetic to our cause, and they invited him to the family home. On the following day I asked Tim how he had fared.

"I'm not going again," he told me, rather bluntly. I asked him why.

"They don't trust me," he said. I had to press him for the reason.

"How long did you stay?" I asked him.

"Oh, I stayed all the evening," he said, "but they never left me in the room alone. Every time someone went out someone else came in, and stayed until the others came back."

My friend denied all knowledge of this, and was very concerned, but no amount of persuasion could coax Tim to go again. He had never been guilty of petty theft, but it indicates how ultra-sensitive are their reactions to any form of mistrust.

Adullam Homes are not homes with a capital "H". They are usually quite inconspicuous, two or three bedroomed terraced houses, comfortably, but not lavishly furnished. We cannot hope to compete with some of the amenities provided in our more modern prisons, such as swimming-pools, billiard and snooker tables, and TV lounges, up-to-date kitchens and excellent cuisine. We do, however, offer a home where they may live their own lives, free of all semblance of authority, and where they can again renew their self-respect, and re-establish themselves in society. We do not inflict on them a set of rules, to be kept "or else" . . . They know that we expect certain standards of conduct, and that we have "unwritten laws" which must not be broken. With the odd isolated exception, they adhere and acquiesce. We have four deputy managers in Liverpool and Birmingham, three of whom have first-hand knowledge of prison life. They make daily contact with the homes, not so much to supervise, as to counsel and assist where needed. They are men who understand and appreciate the problems and the set-backs.

Our best efforts however, and those of a thousand probation officers throughout the land, need to be supplemented by the care and compassion of sincere Christian folk – ordinary people like you and me, who will follow the example of the Master. He was not ashamed to mix with the social outcasts of His day, and to ignore the contempt and criticism of ecclesiastical respectability. He ate the same food, and sat at the same tables.

Our prisons are bursting at the seams. Tomorrow, and every day, the gates will open, and another lonely prisoner will be released upon an unfriendly world to face its condemnation and rejection. Maybe they have robbed us, and outraged all our sense of decency and morality, and maybe they have done it again and again. They are the "lepers" of our society. Are we to join the raucous chorus, and cry "unclean, unclean", and leave them to their despair, "outside the camp"?

Redemption cannot be mass-produced. Every man or woman in our care will at times need individual and personal attention. Many times our efforts to befriend them have been thwarted by jealousy, and a demand for our whole unshared concern. They need to be assured of the sincerity of our feeling for them, and that they really matter. Their desire to monopolise our time and attention is symptomatic of a deep hunger for someone to care.

"I've always had to work hard for my living," says the man of the world. "Why should I waste my time and money on a thriftless law-breaker?"

Why indeed? They have alienated all our charitable instincts, and all our goodwill by their anti-social behaviour. They're surely no longer worthy of our consideration. This reasoning is rational and logical by worldly standards. Sadly it would also seem to be the answer of the Christian church with certain stimulating exceptions.

It is no fault of the child that it is born into a loveless home, to a drunken father, to a shiftless mother, to an upbringing of abuse and ill-treatment. It is no fault of theirs if they are placed in an institution where nobody really cares what happens to them as long as they conform to certain rules. Surely to remember this, is to soften our hearts as we see him leaving those high and uninviting walls.

The ever-escalating crime rate, and the over-crowded prisons, the increase in juvenile delinquency, these are urgent social problems which are no longer the exclusive concern of either local or national government. They concern all of us, you and me, and we must be prepared to shoulder our share of the responsibility. We need to become personally involved, if we have any pretensions to a living Christian faith.

> David therefore departed thence, and escaped to the cave of Adullam: . . . And everyone that was in distress, and everyone that was in debt, and everyone that was discontented, gathered themselves unto him; and he became a captain over them . . . (1 Samuel 22: 1,2)

At our modern Cave of Adullam, we have many that are in debt (with unpaid fines and arrears), many that are in distress, and very many that are discontented. We have ex-prisoners, men who are enslaved by drink or drugs, men who are bound and fettered by their own unbridled passions. They have read our tracts, heard our counselling, received clothing and food and shelter. It is not sufficient. They need *love*, Christ's love, the self-effacing, self-denying and all embracing love. The need to see it in you and me, as we open our hearts and our homes, and bring them the hope of a new and better life, and liberation from their chains. We, too, have travelled the same road, and we have found a deliverance, and the answer to the inarticulate cry of the soul SET ME FREE.

> Down in the human heart,
> Crushed by the tempter,
>   Feelings lie buried, that grace can restore.
> Touched by a loving hand,
> Wakened by kindness,
>   Chords that were broken, will vibrate once more.

> (Fanny J. Crosby)

ABOUT ADULLAM

Our Values

Striving for Excellence
Integrity and Fairness
Valuing the Individual

What We Do
Adullam works with some of the most vulnerable and excluded people in society today and we offer hope and dignity through quality housing and support to people in the following client groups:

- Young, single, homeless people
- Young people leaving care
- Ex-offenders and those at risk of offending
- Homeless people
- People living with HIV/AIDS
- People fleeing domestic violence
- Vulnerable mothers and their children
- People recovering from drug and alcohol addiction
- People living with mental health problems

- Vulnerable excluded families
- Refugees and asylum seekers
- Young men at risk of becoming involved in the gun and gang culture

Adullam provides high quality accommodation in hostels, self-contained flats, bedsits, and two- or three-bedroomed homes. In addition we work with private rental agencies, local authorities and other registered providers to further enhance the accommodation available to meet the ever changing needs of the people we support.

We are actively looking to further increase our owned stock through the purchase of existing housing and/or new-build properties.

Social Enterprise

Adullam has a social enterprise scheme called matt25 which supports, trains and mentors our residents and service users in all housing association disciplines. Accredited through the Open College Network it is our goal for all Adullam clients to find permanent employment following their training and work experience, whereby they have the opportunity to obtain NVQ qualifications.

Investor in Excellence

Awarded the Investor in Excellence accreditation in February 2009, and since re-accredited we are proud of this achievement as it shows our commitment to quality for all the services we provide.

Investor in People

Awarded Investor in People Bronze award in 2011, we are proud to say that we really do value our individuals. We aim to improve on our achievement year on year.

Resident Involvement

Resident involvement plays a large part in how our services are developed in order to improve our work further whilst fully meeting the needs of our stakeholders, residents and service users.

We offer training and mentoring in order to facilitate our residents and service users to attend meetings throughout the Association.

Friends of Adullam

Friends of Adullam is a purposeful way of building links with the wider community so that we can offer the best support and opportunities for vulnerable people. Friends may include; local churches, businesses, clubs, charities and other individuals or groups.

The group was set up in May 2008 and the number of our Friends has been growing steadily since then. Friends are linked to our projects across the country and provide additional opportunities and support to our residents on a long-term basis. Our residents typically stay with us for a maximum of two years before moving on to independent living. Through our Friends we are seeing opportunities of employment and education, but most of all residents are finding friends on a long-term basis for when they do move on.